FLAGSHIP HISTORYMAKERS

PHILIP II

SHEILA RANDALL

An imprint of HarperCollins*Publishers*

Dedication
To Richard, Susannah and Nicola.

Published by HarperCollins*Publishers* Ltd
77–85 Fulham Palace Road
London
W6 8JB

Browse the complete Collins catalogue at
www.collinseducation.com

© HarperCollins*Publishers* Ltd 2004
First published 2004

ISBN 000 717325 3

Sheila Randall asserts the moral right to be
identified as the author of this work.

British Library Cataloguing in Publication Data. A
catalogue record for this book is available from the
British Library.

Series commissioned by Graham Bradbury
Project management by Will Chuter/Marie Insall
Edited by Hayley Willer
Book and cover design by Derek Lee
Map artwork by Richard Morris
Picture research by Celia Dearing
Index by Marie Lorimer
Production by Sarah Robinson
Printed and bound by Martins, Berwick upon Tweed

ACKNOWLEDGEMENTS

The Publishers would like to thank the following
for permission to reproduce extracts from their
books:

Yale University Press for an extract from *The Grand
Strategy of Philip II*, by G. Parker (1998).

The Publishers would like to thank the following
for permission to reproduce pictures on these pages
T=Top, B=Bottom

Photo akg-images, London 20, Auto-de-Fe on the
Plaza Mayor in Madrid 1683 (oil on canvas) by
Francisco Rizi 36, photo akg-images,
London/Joseph Martin: Antonio Perez (oil on
canvas) by Alonzo Sanchez Coello 15, photo
akg-images, London/Erich Lessing: Joanna the Mad
c. 1496 (oil on panel) by Juan de Flandes 19;
Archivo General de Simancas, *Estado 431/16* 26;
www.bridgeman.co.uk/Museo de Santa Cruz/Toledo,
Spain: Don John of Austria (oil on canvas) Italian
School 10, www.bridgeman.co.uk/Philip Mould,
Historical Portraits Ltd, London: Alessandro
Farnese (oil on panel) Dutch School 12T,
www.bridgeman.co.uk/Gemaldelgalerie, Kassel,
Germany: William of Orange 1555–56 (oil on
canvas) by Giacomo Antonio Moro 12B,
www.bridgeman.co.uk/Lobkowicz Collections,
Nelahozeves Castle, Czech Republic: Don Carlos
(oil on panel) after Sofonisba Anguissola, Alonzo
Sanchez Coello 16,
www.bridgeman.co.uk/Prado, Madrid, Spain: The
Garden of Earthly Delights, Allegory of Luxury,
c. 1500 (oil on panel) central panel of triptych, by
Hieronymus Bosch 33,
www.bridgeman.co.uk/Private Collection/Ken Welsh
38; © National Maritime Museum, London: The
Battle of Lepanto (oil on canvas) by H. Letter 53,
Spanish Armada, Adams chart 8 (detail) 57; National
Portrait Gallery, London: Philip II, King of Spain by
an unknown artist *c.* 1580 (oil on canvas) 7.

Cover picture: Mary Evans Picture Library

You might also like to visit
www.harpercollins.co.uk
The book lovers' website

Contents

Why do historians differ?

THE purpose of the Flagship Historymakers series is to explore the main debates surrounding a number of key individuals in British, European and American History.

Each book begins with a chronology of the significant events in the life of the particular individual, and an outline of the person's career. The book then examines in greater detail three of the most important and controversial issues in the life of the individual – issues that continue to attract differing views from historians, and that feature prominently in examination syllabuses in A-level History and beyond.

Each of these issue sections provides students with an overview of the main arguments put forward by historians. By posing key questions, these sections aim to help students to think through the areas of debate and to form their own judgements on the evidence. It is important, therefore, for students to understand why historians differ in their views on past events and, in particular, on the role of individuals in past events.

The study of history is an ongoing debate about events in the past. Although factual evidence is the essential ingredient of history, it is the *interpretation* of factual evidence that forms the basis for historical debate. The study of how and why historians differ in their various interpretations is termed 'historiography'.

Historical debate can occur for a wide variety of reasons.

Insufficient evidence

In some cases there is insufficient evidence to provide a definitive conclusion. In attempting to 'fill the gaps' where factual evidence is unavailable, historians use their professional judgement to make 'informed comments' about the past.

New evidence

As new evidence comes to light, an historian today may have more information on which to base judgements than historians in the past. For instance, the vast Spanish Government archive at Simancas and the Zabálburu library in Madrid only became accessible to scholars after the end of the Franco regime in 1975 and the establishment of a democratic system in Spain.

A 'philosophy' of history?

Many historians have a specific view of history that will affect the way they make their historical judgements. For instance, Marxist historians – who take their view from the writings of Karl Marx, the founder of modern socialism – believe that society has always been made up of competing economic and social classes. They also place considerable importance on economic reasons behind human decision-making. Therefore, a Marxist historian looking at an historical issue may take a completely different viewpoint to a non-Marxist historian.

The role of the individual

Some historians have seen past history as being largely moulded by the acts of specific individuals. Philip II, William of Orange and Henry of Navarre are seen as individuals whose personality and beliefs changed the course of 16th-century European History. Other historians have tended to play down the role of individuals; instead, they highlight the importance of more general social, economic and political change. Rather than seeing William of Orange as an individual who changed the course of Dutch history, these historians tend to see him as representing the views of a broader group of individuals, such as those urban 'politiques' who placed the welfare of the state before their religious beliefs.

Placing different emphases on the same historical evidence

Even if historians do not possess different philosophies of history or place different emphasis on the role of the individual, it is still possible for them to disagree in one very important way. This is that they may place different emphases on aspects of the same factual evidence. As a result, History should be seen as a subject that encourages debate about the past, based on historical evidence.

Historians will always differ

Historical debate is, in its nature, continuous. What today may be an accepted view about a past event may well change in the future, as the debate continues.

Timeline: Philip II's life

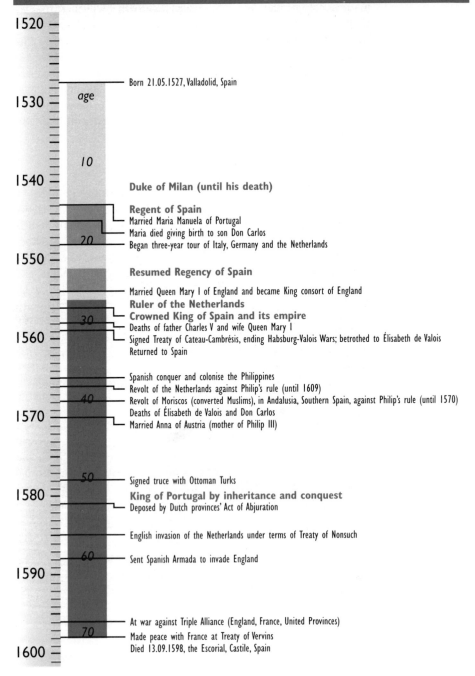

1520 —

1530 — *age*

— Born 21.05.1527, Valladolid, Spain

10

1540 —
Duke of Milan (until his death)

Regent of Spain
Married Maria Manuela of Portugal
Maria died giving birth to son Don Carlos
20 Began three-year tour of Italy, Germany and the Netherlands

1550 —

Resumed Regency of Spain

Married Queen Mary I of England and became King consort of England
Ruler of the Netherlands
Crowned King of Spain and its empire
30 Deaths of father Charles V and wife Queen Mary I
1560 — Signed Treaty of Cateau-Cambrésis, ending Habsburg-Valois Wars; betrothed to Élisabeth de Valois
Returned to Spain

Spanish conquer and colonise the Philippines
Revolt of the Netherlands against Philip's rule (until 1609)
40 Revolt of Moriscos (converted Muslims), in Andalusia, Southern Spain, against Philip's rule (until 1570)
1570 — Deaths of Élisabeth de Valois and Don Carlos
Married Anna of Austria (mother of Philip III)

50 Signed truce with Ottoman Turks
1580 — **King of Portugal by inheritance and conquest**
Deposed by Dutch provinces' Act of Abjuration

English invasion of the Netherlands under terms of Treaty of Nonsuch

60 Sent Spanish Armada to invade England
1590 —

At war against Triple Alliance (England, France, United Provinces)
70 Made peace with France at Treaty of Vervins
1600 — Died 13.09.1598, the Escorial, Castile, Spain

Philip II's favourite portrait, aged 53, as conqueror of Portugal. His son Philip III was only 2 years old.

Philip II: a brief biography

How did Philip II make history?

Philip II (1527–98) ruled Spain during its **Golden Age**, when Castilians and Aragonese first called themselves 'Spaniards'. He was the scourge of the English for sending **the Armada**, and of the Netherlanders for crushing their legal, judicial and political privileges. The forbidding granite powerhouse of his vast empire, **the Escorial**, stands a testimony to his austerity. Champion of the **Counter-Reformation**, he trusted that his cause and God's were the same. His enemies declared him a tyrant, who imposed Catholic orthodoxy through war and the Spanish Inquisition. His character was full of paradoxes: determined yet indecisive, pious yet cruel, just yet above the law. His four wives and two daughters adored him, yet he was suspected of murdering his eldest son. He ruled 16 million Europeans, including inhabitants of the Netherlands and parts of Italy. Globally he ruled 40 million subjects, including inhabitants of the Americas, the East Indies and outposts in North Africa. Europeans coveted his silver fleets, which monopolised world trade, yet he declared bankruptcy four times and left his successor an immense debt. His contemporaries feared the power of his empire 'over which the sun never ceased to shine', yet his mismanagement of it inaugurated the 'decline of Spain' in the 17th century.

Apprenticeship

Philip was born at Valladolid on 21 May 1527, son of Habsburg Emperor Charles V and Isabella of Portugal. Fifteen days earlier (during the **Habsburg-Valois Wars)**, his father's Lutheran troops held Pope Clement VII prisoner as they brutally **sacked** Rome. Even before he married, Charles had signed over his Austrian dynastic lands to his brother Ferdinand, leaving Spain as the heart of Philip's inheritance. Philip was brought up in Castile by Catholic clerics chosen by his pious mother, who died before his twelfth birthday. They gave him a thirst for knowledge and a love of mathematics and science. He was personally inclined towards art, architecture, music and the occult. Unlike his father, he failed to master foreign languages, learning a little Portuguese but favouring Castilian. He played the guitar and danced well. He did not sing but did enjoy plainsong and choral music. Recurrent illness led to expectations that he would not live long, but by 16 years old he was Regent of Spain in his father's absence, dutifully obeying his *Instructions*. One of these *Instructions* advised abstinence from excessive sexual pleasure. After only 18 months of marriage to Maria of Portugal, her death in childbirth made Philip a father and a widower by the age of 18.

Early travels and accession

Heretics: Christians whose beliefs conflict with official Catholic belief and tradition — beliefs that were punishable, under heresy laws, by excommunication and burning at the stake.

From 1548, Philip enjoyed a three-year tour of Italy, Germany and the Netherlands, encountering his future subjects and gaining first-hand experience of **heretics**. In 1554, aged 27, he dutifully married Mary Tudor, 11 years her junior, but she died four years later without the longed-for Habsburg heir to encircle France. In 1556, his father's abdication made him King of a vast inheritance (see map opposite) gained by marriage and conquest. His reign started auspiciously with victory over France at St Quentin, on St Lawrence's day 1557, which he commemorated by building the Escorial. Bankrupt, due to inherited war debts, he made peace at Cateau-Cambrésis in 1559, confirming Spain's mastery of Italy and making the 13-year-old Élisabeth de Valois his third wife. She was to give him two beautiful daughters, Isabella and Catalina. At 32 years old, Philip returned to Castile, establishing Madrid as his administrative centre in 1561. He never left the Iberian Peninsula again.

Ottoman Turks: from Asia Minor, successive Ottoman sultans expanded their Muslim empire throughout the Middle East and Egypt, capturing Constantinople (Istanbul) (1453). Land advance gained them part of Hungary, and led them to besiege Vienna (1529), posing a major threat to Habsburg and Catholic European territories. Ottoman fleets dominated the Eastern Mediterranean and pushed westwards, wintering in Toulon (1543/4).

Conflicts of priority

Philip's departure from the Netherlands in 1559 left seeds of discontent that flared into revolt by 1566. In Spain, factions vied for power at court and groups of heretics were uncovered. Philip maintained religious orthodoxy through Castilian officials, personally controlling an inherited conciliar system and Inquisition. The Peruvian silver mines of Potosi provided credit for loans to finance his policies. Philip prioritised defence of Spain from the **Ottoman Turks**, who were advancing towards the Western Mediterranean and who were collaborating with **Barbary corsairs** in attacks on Spanish transport and commerce en route to Italian ports. Philip feared that they might seize vital corn imports and sever communications with the **Spanish Road**. Moriscos (Muslim **fifth-columnists**) also endangered Catholicism. Disaster at Djerba (1560) and the siege and relief of Malta (1565) distracted Philip from crushing unrest in the Netherlands. Only the death of Ottoman Sultan Suleiman the Magnificent (1566) enabled the despatch of the Duke of Alva's army to Brussels.

Barbary corsairs: Muslim pirates led by Barbarossa (Red Beard); vassals of the Ottoman Sultan. They controlled Algiers (1516) and, briefly, Tunis (1534/5). They frequently raided the Spanish Balearic Islands and Eastern mainland ports.

In 1568, the sudden deaths of his wife Élisabeth, aged just 22, and his only son Don Carlos, aged 23, coincided with the Moriscos

Spanish Road: military supply route, connecting Spain with the Netherlands via Genoa and the Alps.

Fifth-columnists: traitors or spies within society, working for the enemy.

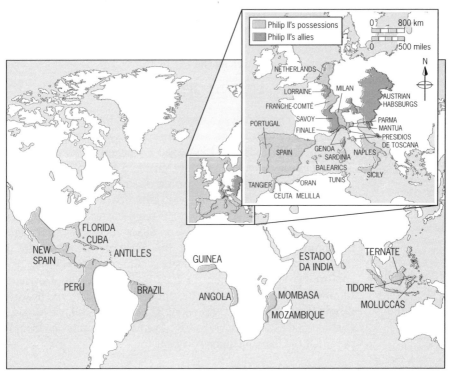

The main map shows Philip II's global empire. His European and North African territories are shown in the inset map.

Revolt and plunged Philip into deep depression. The need for an heir led to his fourth marriage, at the age of 43, to his niece Anna of Austria, who was half his age. In 1571, his half-brother **Don John of Austria** led a Holy League fleet that destroyed the Ottoman navy at the Battle of Lepanto. Philip celebrated the victory by commissioning a large painting entitled *Spain Coming to the Aid of Religion*. Bankrupted again (1575), his overstretched, unpaid troops mutinied, enflaming the Netherlands. At 51 years old, his joy at the birth of his heir Philip III was marred by his implication in the murder of an official suspected of treason.

Don John of Austria (1547–78)
Illegitimate son of Charles V and Barbara Blomberg, Don John was brought up secretly in Spain and only acknowledged in 1554. Twenty years Philip's junior, he first met Philip in 1559.

Energetic and handsome, Don John was popular and had several illegitimate children. Philip may have envied him and viewed him as a rival. Don John was commander of the Spanish Mediterranean fleet, the army which crushed the Moriscos Revolt with heavy atrocities, and the Holy League fleet, which won the Battle of Lepanto (1571). He became governor general of the Netherlands in 1575, and died of plague there on 1 October 1578.

Understanding Philip II

■ **A man of deep Catholic faith**, whose treasured collection of 7422 relics included 12 entire bodies, 144 complete heads and 306 limbs of saints.

■ **A man with a rigid sense of duty to God, nation and family**, who deeply loved his wife Anna, and who wrote loving letters to his daughters.

■ **A man who refused to delegate**, who was inflexible and resigned to failure in times of crisis.

■ **A man who never betrayed emotion or intention**, causing suspicions of his double-dealing.

■ **A man with an obsessive fear of failure**, he agonised over decisions. He allowed a relative to carry his baby son to the baptismal font even though he had wanted to so much that he had practised with a doll of similar size and weight for days.

■ **A man with an obsession for micromanaging detail**, who poured out his thoughts on his vast paperwork even though he disliked discussion.

■ **A cultured and educated man**, who sponsored artists (such as Titian, Coello and Moro), histories, geographies, surveys and maps.

■ **A man who enjoyed gardens and hunting**, who brought Flemish gardeners and shrubs to Spain, and who housed exotic animals in his menageries.

■ **A man with a wry sense of humour**, who enjoyed entertainment by acrobats, buffoons and dwarves.

■ **A man who suffered many illnesses**, including bowel problems, arthritis, kidney disease and gout.

'What his father won by the sword, he preserves with the pen.'
Francesco Vendramino, Venetian ambassador to Madrid, 1593

Alexander Farnese, Duke of Parma (1545–92) Son of Philip II's illegitimate half-sister, Margaret of Parma (Regent of the Netherlands 1559–67). The Duke of Parma was made military commander in the Netherlands in 1578 and recovered a great deal of rebel-held territory, until ordered by Philip to meet the Armada in 1588 and fight in France. He died there in 1592.

A change of direction

After Don John's death from plague (1578), Philip replaced him with **Alexander Farnese, Duke of Parma**, who began to reconquer the Netherlands despite continued English and French interference. Elizabeth I encouraged English **privateers** to prey on Spanish Caribbean possessions, and Sir Francis Drake audaciously raided Spanish ports. Philip plotted in favour of Mary Queen of Scots, threatening to invade England.

Privateers: pirates.

To the Pope's disgust, Philip signed a pragmatic truce with the Turks (1578). In 1580, he acquired Portugal, uniting all Iberia under his rule but disquieting his enemies. His shift of priority was shown in outlawing the Dutch rebel leader, **William of Orange**, offering a reward and ennoblement to his assassin. By the **Act of Abjuration** (1581), the United Provinces renounced allegiance to Philip.

Act of Abjuration: Act passed in July 1581, in which the States General of the United Provinces (Brabant, Gelderland, Flanders, Holland, Zeeland, Utrecht, Friesland, Tournai and Mechelen) solemnly deposed Philip II as their ruler.

Reputation in danger

Orange was assassinated and the Duke of Anjou, Catholic supporter of the Calvinist Dutch rebels, died (1584). France had been too preoccupied with civil war to threaten Spain, but **Huguenot** leader, Henry of Navarre, now succeeded Anjou as heir to the French

Huguenot: French heretic.

William of Orange (1533–84)

William of Nassau, Prince of Orange, had been a close advisor to Charles V. In 1561, outraged at his removal from the Council of State by Philip II, he successfully campaigned for the removal of Cardinal Granvelle, Philip's minister, along with Counts Egmont and Hoorn and Baron Montigny. They demanded relaxation of the heresy laws in the Netherlands. William held aloof from the Netherlands Revolt in 1566, but fled to Germany when the Duke of Alva's army approached in 1567. He was sentenced to death in his absence by Alva's Council of Troubles. In 1568, he led an abortive attempt to invade the Netherlands with French help. He converted to Calvinism in 1573 and attracted foreign aid. Philip became obsessed with the thought that the revolt would only end if Orange were removed. In 1580, Philip declared Orange an outlaw. William replied with the *Apology* (1581) to justify his involvement in the Revolt of the Netherlands, declaring Philip II a tyrant and murderer. In 1584, Orange was assassinated by a Catholic fanatic.

throne. Philip tried to prevent his accession by aiding the French Catholic League, with money and troops, in the Treaty of Joinville (1584).

The Duke of Parma's military success against the weakened Dutch rebels brought English troops to their aid, invading the Netherlands under the terms of the Treaty of Nonsuch (1585). Years of tense peace with England ended, and Philip's Armada assembled in Lisbon. The Pope promised Philip one million ducats, payable when troops landed on English soil.

Bad luck dogged preparations. Sir Francis Drake burnt ships and supplies in Cadiz (1587), Admiral Santa Cruz died (February 1588), and the Duke of Medina Sidonia was a poor replacement. The plans were known throughout Europe, putting Philip's reputation at stake, but he was intransigent. The disciplined crescent of ships in the Channel struck awe into Englishmen's hearts, but **fireships** and North Sea storms scattered the Armada, wasting ten million ducats. Perhaps God's cause and Philip's were not always the same. Queen Elizabeth's commemorative medal recorded, 'God blew and they were scattered.'

Fireships: English ships filled with tar, set on fire and sent among the Spanish fleet to cause panic.

The crises of the 1590s

The 1590s saw a catalogue of disasters: revolt in Aragon 1591; plague in Madrid; and military stalemate in the Netherlands after an angry Parma, poised for victory, was withdrawn to meet the Armada and fight in France. Henry of Navarre converted to Catholicism to be crowned King of France in 1593. Philip stubbornly fought on, disobeying the Pope and claiming the French crown for his daughter Isabella. Spain faced a Triple Alliance of French, English and Dutch, and two further failed Armadas. Bankruptcy forced Philip to end the French War at the Treaty of Vervins (1598). Philip II died in the Escorial on 13 September 1598, after months of excruciating illness, clutching his beloved religious relics. Spain's Golden Age was over.

1 Was Philip II a cruel tyrant or a 'Paper King'?

To what extent was he a cruel tyrant?

To what extent did he centralise his power?

How far was his power limited by an obsession with paperwork?

Framework of events

1543	Gonzalo Perez appointed royal secretary (until 1566)
	Factional rivalry at court
1561	Madrid becomes administrative centre
1563	Construction of the Escorial begins
1564	Philip II is forced to withdraw Cardinal Granvelle from the Netherlands
1566	Outbreak of the Netherlands Revolt against Philip's rule (until 1609)
	Cardinal Espinosa appointed President of the Council of Castile and Inquisitor-General
	Antonio Perez and Gabriel de Zayas appointed royal secretaries
1568	Council of Troubles orders executions of Counts Egmont and Hoorn
	Deaths of Don Carlos and Élisabeth de Valois
	Outbreak of Moriscos Revolt against Philip's rule (until 1570)
1570	On Philip's orders, Baron Montigny executed at Simancas prison
1572	Philip dismisses Cardinal Espinosa
	Mateo Vazquez appointed royal secretary (until 1585)
1578	Juan de Escobedo murdered
1579	Arrest of Antonio Perez
	Cardinal Granvelle appointed head of Council of State
1580	Philip annexes Portugal and its empire
1585	Philip expands junta system to speed up administrative decisions
1590	Cortes grants *millones* tax with more than 100 conditions
1591	Aragon Revolt

Antonio Perez (1540–1611)
Antonio Perez was the illegitimate son of Philip's secretary Gonzalo Perez, and succeeded him as royal secretary. He assumed leadership of the Eboli faction (1573) on the death of the Prince of Eboli, whose widow, beautiful one-eyed Ana de Mendoza, may have had an affair with Perez. Imprisoned in Madrid (1579) for Escobedo's murder, he escaped in 1590 and stirred up the Aragon Revolt (1591). He escaped to France, smeared Philip's reputation, and died there in 1611.

'No character was ever drawn by different historians in more opposite colours than Philip II,' wrote Robert Watson, in *The History of the Reign of Philip the Second, King of Spain* (1794), in an age when history was considered the product of great men and villains. Philip II's Castilian subjects saw him as a just, pious and prudent King. Spanish historians from Cabrera in 1619 to Ballesteros in 1947 thought the King embodied the national spirit. But to many of Philip's subjects, he was a remote and arrogant foreigner, whose rule over them resulted from dynastic marriage or the fortuitous gains of individual conquistadors. The national awareness that characterised the 16th century encouraged his subjects to defend their customs, traditions and privileges against foreign domination. Catholic resurgence against a tide of **Protestant secession** placed Philip at the forefront of a militant Counter-Reformation movement, which alarmed his enemies and instigated bitter attacks on his character.

His reputation was denigrated most luridly in the emotive words of American historian John Motley, in *The Rise of the Dutch Republic* (1856). Nineteenth-century nationalism and American independence provide the backdrop, and Motley's Protestant beliefs the enthusiasm, for his study of Philip's tyranny and oppression. Although thoroughly researched, the book used unreliable Dutch propaganda and the reminiscences of Philip's disgraced secretary **Antonio Perez**. Motley deepened the **Black Legend** and accused Philip of 'monstrous crimes'.

Protestant secession: many Protestant rulers withdrew, or seceded, from papal control and set up state churches.

Black Legend: bitter propaganda that claimed Spain aimed to rule the world. It first arose in late 15th-century Italy where Spanish troops fought to control Naples. Harsh use of the Inquisition against Spanish Moors and Jews, and atrocities perpetrated by Spanish conquistadors in Mexico and Peru after 1519, added to the myth. Philip II's enemies boosted the legend with accusations against Philip himself.

To what extent was Philip II a cruel tyrant?

Absolutism or tyranny?

Absolutism: ab solutus – literally, monarchs absolved (excused) from obedience to the law as authors of it.

Absolutism was attributed to many 16th-century rulers, recognising their power of life and death over every citizen in the interests of state security and natural justice. It made them above the law and answerable to God alone. Historians have consistently agreed that Philip's power was theoretically absolute, but they disagree on whether he acted in the interests of his subjects. Before the 20th century, most historians felt he acted from self-interest, supporting Spanish theorist Pedro Agustín Morla, who stated, in 1599, 'Absolute power is, more exactly, tyranny, and was invented by the flatterers of kings.'

Was Philip II the 'Most Just of Rulers'?

Philip II's Castilian subjects loved him as the 'Most Just of Rulers', shown by the cheering crowds that stretched well over a mile when he returned from Lisbon in 1583 after three years absence. Philip saw himself as God's instrument, charged with a duty to defend his lands and administer justice, fulfilling both Castilian tradition of the king as lawgiver, and his father's *Instructions* (1543) to 'Impart justice in such a manner that the bad find you terrible and the good find you benign.' As lawgiver, he codified all laws in force in Castile and 300 royal proclamations in *The Laws of the Realm* (1569); he expanded the impartial and independent legal system with new high courts of appeal ('audiencias'). His codified Portuguese laws (1593) were in force until 1640. Many historians cite Philip's instruction in a financial case – 'Take note that in case of doubt, the verdict must always go against me' – to point out the King's interventions to soften the rigour of the law: 'justice tempered with mercy'.

Philip's reputation for justice also depended on even-handed punishment of the guilty: from the lowly to the highest Castilian grandee. However, when his subjects openly criticised the solitary confinement of his son **Don Carlos** without trial, Philip silenced them without explanation. His **dissimulation** strategy enabled his enemies to construct the myth of the cruel and tyrannical father.

Dissimulation: secrecy and concealment. Philip thought it essential strategy not to betray his intentions or emotions.

Don Carlos (1545–68)

Born on 8 July 1545 to 17 year-old Maria of Portugal, who died of a haemorrhage four days later. Don Carlos was born physically and mentally handicapped and, in childhood, also displayed impulsive, aggressive and violent behaviour. In 1562, a fall down stairs caused him brain damage, leaving him in a coma. Flemish anatomist Andreas Vesalius carried out a trepanning operation to save his life (a hole was drilled in his skull to release the pressure – a procedure also used to treat insanity). After his recovery his behaviour deteriorated. In violent rages, he threw a servant out of a window, attacked the Duke of Alva with a knife and, when riding, lacerated his horses' sides with his spurs. In 1567, he threatened his father's life and conspired with his uncle Don John of Austria and Baron Montigny.

Philip had Don Carlos arrested late at night on 18 January 1568 and imprisoned. Rumours circulated that during his confinement he ate excessive meals, drank large quantities of ice-cold water and slept in a bed full of ice. His sickly constitution collapsed under the strain, causing his self-inflicted death on 24 July 1568.

Baron Montigny (1527–70) Floris de Montmorency, Baron Montigny, was younger brother of Count Hoorn — both were knights	of the Golden Fleece. A cousin had commanded the French army defeated by Philip II at St Quentin in 1557. Montigny was sent to Madrid in 1566, to request	relaxation of the Netherlands heresy laws, but stopped in France, arousing Philip's fears of a conspiracy. In September 1567, after Alva's despatch	to Brussels, Montigny was imprisoned, and garrotted (strangled with a knotted rope), at Philip's instruction, on 16th October 1570.

Council of Troubles: nicknamed the 'Council of Blood', a special tribunal set up by the Duke of Alva in Brussels to try those implicated in the Netherlands Revolt of 1566.

Order of the Golden Fleece: a Netherlands chivalric order; membership of which conferred special privileges on its knights, such as the right to trial by fellow members.

Fueros: local jurisdictions and privileges.

Justiciar: chief justice.

Claims of tyranny also surround Philip's decision to have **Baron Montigny** secretly garrotted in Simancas castle (1570); a death he publicly attributed to natural causes. In 1568, the Duke of Alva's **Council of Troubles** in Brussels had executed Counts Egmont and Hoorn after trial for treason, in violation of their privileges as knights of the **Order of the Golden Fleece**. Baron Montigny, in Madrid seeking concessions, and William of Orange, in refuge in Germany, were condemned in their absence. Montigny's treason, sentence, suspected conspiracy with Don Carlos and attempt to escape, justified his death for state security. Philip acted secretly to protect his subjects; a public execution would have failed to edify Spaniards and would have merely provoked reprisals if carried out in Brussels.

Philip's absolute intervention in the cases of **Juan de Escobedo** (1578) and Antonio Perez (1591) may also be justified for state security. In 1578, Perez claimed that Juan de Escobedo was selling state secrets. The falsity of these accusations was only discovered after Escobedo's murder on Perez's orders and with the King's alleged authorisation. Historians interpret Philip's inaction in seeking the murderer as an admission of guilt, although Henry Kamen, in *Philip of Spain* (1997), argues that the King only intervened personally in cases of alleged treason. The King violated Aragon's **fueros** by trumping up heresy charges against Perez, to bring him to justice, causing revolt in Aragon (1591). Philip sent in a Castilian army and executed **Justiciar** Lanuza without trial.

Was Philip II guilty of 'monstrous crimes'?

Scottish Presbyterian Robert Watson, in *The History of the Reign of Philip the Second, King of Spain* (1794), describes Philip's 'odious and shocking crimes' as incest, murder, lechery and sodomy. His

Juan de Escobedo (1530–78) Juan de Escobedo was secretary to Don John of Austria after 1575, and a	member of the Eboli court faction. Philip II's corrupt royal secretary Antonio Perez schemed against Escobedo and Don John,	alleging their treason, which Escobedo discovered on a visit to Madrid (1577). Escobedo was murdered on the orders of Perez (1578)	before he could expose the duplicity of Perez, who claimed he had papers proving the King's complicity.

source was William of Orange's *Apology* (1581), which was based on rumours spread by French Ambassador Raimond de Fourquevaux, among others, following the deaths of Philip's son and heir Don Carlos and Philip's third wife Élisabeth de Valois, within three months of each other (1568). Their closeness in age – Don Carlos, at 23 years old, a year older than his stepmother – encouraged rumours of a romantic liaison and a jealous, murderous father. Philip's accustomed secrecy fuelled the myth.

John Motley, in *The Rise of the Dutch Republic* (1856), left a vivid and lasting image of:

> A superhuman monster: cruel, intolerant, grossly immoral, a complete tyrant and hypocrite, without a single virtue, and perhaps lacking *every* vice only because it is not permitted to human nature to attain perfection even in evil.

Schiller's play *Don Carlos* (1787) and Verdi's opera of the same title (1867) perpetuated the image. Leopold von Ranke's 'scientific' history *The Ottoman and the Spanish Empires in the Sixteenth and Seventeenth Centuries* (1843) first repeated Venetian ambassadors' gossip that 'It was not far from the King's smile to his dagger.' Cecil Jean Cadoux, in *Philip of Spain and the Netherlands* (1947), comments:

> There is nothing unlikely in Philip having secretly had any person put out of the way, whose life he regarded as prejudicial to the security and well-being of his throne, his person, or his Church.

However, except for the use of secrecy, this was true of all 16th-century rulers, including Elizabeth I.

As for Philip II's cruelty, even Antonio Perez recorded that the King 'wept three days for his son' after his sudden death in custody, and contemporaries recorded the King's 'profound grief' at the death of his wife Élisabeth in childbirth. James Casey, in 'Philip II of Spain: the Prudent King' in *The Historian* (1998), sums up the general view:

> Historical investigation has dismantled the myth of Don Carlos, replacing the heartless, jealous Philip of literature with the bereaved father, inwardly distraught by his son's madness and death from self-inflicted wounds while in confinement.

Geoffrey Parker, in *The Grand Strategy of Philip II* (1998), illustrates the King's depressed state of mind in a letter written a few months later during the Moriscos Revolt, in which the King confided:

**Joanna the Mad
(1479–1555)**

Philip's grandmother, daughter of Isabella of Castile and Ferdinand of Aragon, and sister of Catherine of Aragon, wife of Henry VIII. At 17 she married Philip 'the Fair' of Burgundy, son of the Habsburg Emperor Maximilian I. Joanna was passionately devoted to her husband and suffered a mental breakdown when he died unexpectedly in 1506, at the age of 28. She repeatedly opened his coffin to look for signs of renewed life, only agreeing to bury him three years later. Her father Ferdinand of Aragon declared her unfit to rule, forcing her to abdicate the throne of Castile in favour of her son Charles V, who was 6 years old at the time. She was confined to Tordesillas monastery, with her daughter Catalina for company, and died 49 years later.

I am no good for the world today, I should be in some other station in life, one less exalted than the one God has given me, which for me alone is terrible.

Historians now accept that Philip II placed the good of the state above family, considering the consequence for Spain of the accession of Don Carlos and the precedent of **Joanna the Mad**.

William of Orange's *Apology* (1581) was a reply to Philip's edict that outlawed him and placed a price of 25 000 crowns on his head, to try to end the Revolt of the Netherlands. The Dutch also originated the 'Advice of the Inquisition', a supposed royal edict of 1568 (but, in the early 20th century, proven a forgery), sentencing every man, woman and child in the Netherlands to death. John Motley used it to accuse 'the royal criminal called Philip II' of attempted genocide, claiming Philip 'could boast of having strangled, drowned, burned or beheaded somewhat more than 18 000 of his fellow creatures'. Estimates suggest that the Duke of Alva's Council of Troubles executed 1105 Dutch rebels and convicted another 8000 in their absence, and Philip had given the Duke a 'free hand' to restore order for his royal visit, which never took place. Alva's hard-line approach was to make everyone live 'in constant fear of the roof breaking down over his head', exaggerated in its significance as 'ghoulish' and compared with 20th-century dictatorship, by Victor G. Kiernan in *State and Society in Europe, 1550–1650* (1980).

In his last testament, the only occasion on which he referred to himself as 'absolute', Philip advised his son:

Never condemn a man to death except unhappily or unwillingly, forced by the demands of justice and the necessity for law and order.

This sense of natural justice epitomises Kamen's view, and other historians generally portray Philip II as no more cruel or tyrannical than his contemporaries.

Absolutism versus liberty and privilege

Philip lived in the age of Machiavelli, advocate of 'the end justifies the means'; a time of struggle between absolutism and liberty. Aggaeus van Albada, a Dutch lawyer, justified Philip's deposition in 1581, as a tyrant and oppressor, thus:

Princes were made for the people, the essence of political authority is to foster and protect the common good.

Philip initiated the Duke of Alva's overhaul of the legal system in the Netherlands, to streamline it and introduce new military funding, but this violated provincial customs and privileges.

Two essays, in *The Origins and Development of the Dutch Revolt* (2001), illustrate the argument of absolutism versus liberty and privilege. The first, Martin van Gelderen's 'Theories of Monarchy and Civil Power', identifies a fundamental clash of ideologies between Spain and the Netherlands. While Philip was seen as absolutist, William of Orange's *Apology* focused Dutch views on political power being 'nothing but the right of the common people'. (He had claimed that Philip had misused his God-given power, to oppress his subjects, and that the power to remove him lay with the people.) The second essay, Henk van Nierop's 'Alva's Throne: Making Sense of the Revolt of the Netherlands', explains the Dutch view of 'freedom' as sovereignty spread across different components of the state while the prince respected his subjects' privileges and rights.

These views were revolutionary for the 16th century, repeating the Calvinist 'right of resistance' and Philippe du Plessis-Mornay's *Vindiciae Contra Tyrannos* (1579), a French tract claiming the people's right to resist an evil king. Juan de Mariana, in *De Rege et Regis Institutione* (1599), also claimed this.

Engraving by Frans Hogenberg, showing the Duke of Alva enthroned, with the devil blowing vengeance and blood lust into his ear. A peasant and burgher watch in anguish as he and Granvelle eat the innocent child that represents the Netherlands. Alva's feet rest on the corpses of Egmont and Hoorn.

Geoffrey Parker, in *The Grand Strategy of Philip II* (1998), argues that Philip normally took care to rule through 'established constitutional channels' and, in practice, all 16th-century monarchs swore a coronation oath to defend the privileges of their individual territories. Henry Kamen, in *Philip of Spain* (1997), points out that Philip had a clear sense of responsibility for his subjects: 'The people were not made for the sake of the Prince', Philip admitted, 'but the Prince was instituted for the instance of the people.' The King was aware that effective rule was only possible if he respected the rights and jurisdictions of his provinces, especially after the lesson of the Netherlands. His absolutism existed only on paper.

To what extent did Philip II centralise his power?

Did Philip II centralise his power over Castile?

Fernand Braudel, in *The Mediterranean and the Mediterranean World in the Age of Philip II* (1949) (See **Landmark Study**, below), states that Philip's enemies 'saw him as a spider sitting motionless at the centre of his web', a sedentary monarch. Philip commented, 'Travelling about one's kingdom is neither useful nor decent.' However, Henry Kamen, in *Philip of Spain* (1997), portrays a much more active and cosmopolitan King, who enjoyed entertainment and travelled widely within the Iberian Peninsula. From 1561, Madrid was Philip's administrative centre. His elaborate court of 1500 officials in the Royal Palace at Madrid was supplemented by the Escorial and his private informal retreats (such as Aranjuez, the

---

Landmark Study   The book that changed people's views

F. Braudel, *The Mediterranean and the Mediterranean World in the Age of Philip II*
(First published in French 1949, translation published 1972 by HarperCollins)

Fernand Braudel transformed the study and writing of history. Historians had previously based their work on historical events and viewed great men as the agents of change. Braudel's 'total history' is shaped by a variety of linear human currents, rhythms and structures. He dismisses events as 'momentary outbursts' and believes that the individual is a weak agent of change, acting within a strong structure.

The Mediterranean and the Mediterranean World in the Age of Philip II, based on years of research, was written from memory during Braudel's five years as a German prisoner of war. Part 1 explores the environment: the impact on the history of the Mediterranean of the peninsulas, the seas and coasts, the boundaries and the climate. Part 2 evaluates collective destinies and general trends: the effects on

historical trends of economies, origins of empires, societies, civilisations and forms of war, including piracy. Part 3 discusses events, politics and people, specifically the clash of Spanish and Turkish empires. Braudel's work changed the perception of Philip II to that of a King restricted by his inheritance.

Pardo, and Valsaín near Segovia), in the heart of Castile. This contrasted with the frequent 'progresses' of his great-grandparents, Isabella and Ferdinand, and with his father's itinerant court. In *Early Habsburg Spain, 1517–1598* (1986), A. W. Lovett summarises the change:

> What had been a polyglot empire administered by a migratory court now became Castilian, ruled from a fixed point.

Philip had a deep sense of duty to maintain the Habsburg conciliar system, even though it was not designed for an ever-present monarch (see Habsburg Conciliar System on page 23). However, the system had no central administration, civil service, police force, army or tax framework. In theory, power was centralised in the appropriate council in Madrid, but, in practice, the administrators on the spot ran affairs from day to day. Jurisdictions overlapped, and corruption was endemic within the system. Henry Kamen, in *Philip of Spain* (1997), suggests:

> Many provinces were virtually self-governing, and Spain was no centralised state. Beyond the scope of royal councils, direct royal authority was tenuous, and Philip's autocratic power was that of a **'Paper King'**.

'Paper King': an administrator King too bogged down in paperwork to actively rule his lands.

Traditionally, historians argued that Philip attempted to centralise control of his empire, but this is now a matter of controversy. Even within Castile, centralisation was a struggle against time and distance – access to Madrid was impeded by its situation on a high plateau, by poor roads and provincial barriers. Some historians suggest that Philip did not aim to centralise his power, realising it would be impractical. For example, he allowed Portugal to retain its privileges after its annexation (1580).

Corregidors: Castilian officials – local judges and law officers, who marshalled citizens, provisioned towns and mustered the militia in wartime.

Señorios: grants of land entailing judicial rights.

The duty to implement Philip's policies in Castilian towns lay in the hands of the 66 royal administrators called **corregidors**. They also had a range of local duties, and self-interest often caused them to ignore royal commands and give priority to the interests of local noblemen. Since the 12th century, financial weakness had led monarchs to sell *señorios* throughout large swathes of Castile. These awards gave noblemen great estates with rights to control tenants, justice, taxation, appointments and enlistment in the royal militia. The Duke of Medina Sidonia could boast a private army of 10 000 men.

Castile was traditionally seen as a great power in its own right, but Henry Kamen disputes its economic strength, arguing that the Castilian economy was outside the King's control. Noble exemption

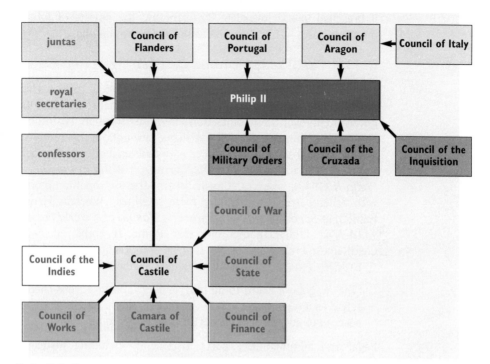

The Spanish Conciliar System under Philip II.

from direct taxes discouraged investment in industry, which would mean loss of noble status. The privileges and power of the **Mesta** also seriously undermined royal power. Philip continued his predecessors' policy of selling royal land, noble titles and estates of the Military Orders, further undermining central control of the localities.

Mesta: sheep owners' union.

Historians traditionally view the Castilian **Cortes** as a docile body, rubber-stamping Philip's edicts and financial demands: a 'subservient tool of monarchical power' argues Peter Pierson in *Philip II of Spain* (1975). The King told them:

Cortes: parliament – the Castilian one represented 80 major towns.

'If I so wish, I shall annul, without the Cortes, any laws made in the Cortes; I shall legislate by decree, and abolish laws by decree.'

Servicio: direct tax.

Millones **tax**: a very unpopular tax, levied directly on basic food such as wine, oil, vinegar and meat, proposed in the Armada year of 1588 and formally agreed in April 1590.

However, in 'Philip II and the Cortes of Castile' in *Past and Present* (1985), Charles Jago establishes that the Cortes was far from compliant when discussing increases in taxation, in a reign when the *servicio* quadrupled. Their attempts to establish 'redress before supply' in 1566/7, and again in the 1570s, were crowned by a victory in the case of the new *millones* tax (1590). Philip was forced to accept more than one hundred legal conditions before it was granted, which, if breached would invalidate it, restricting the powers of future monarchs. Absolutism, even in Castile, had its limitations.

Did he 'Castilianise' beyond Castile?

John Elliott, in *Imperial Spain 1469–1716* (1963), argues that Philip chose the Alva faction's Castilian nationalist solution to government, over the Eboli faction's federalist solution. Historians agree that Philip employed Castilians throughout his empire, provoking opposition among other nationalities. Fernand Braudel, in *The Mediterranean and the Mediterranean World in the Age of Philip II* (1949), observes, 'Castile became the metropolitan power with other parts of the empire mere satellites.' Whereas Henry Kamen, in *Spain's Road to Empire: The Making of a World Power, 1492–1763* (2003), points out that Philip II employed non-Castilians and relied also on the support of local elites.

In 1559, Venetian Ambassador Michele Suriano reported:

'The Aragonese claim to be independent, and to govern themselves as a republic, of which the King is the head. He may not succeed to government unless they have elected him.'

Legal and administrative posts in Aragon, including justiciar, required native birth. Suriano commented:

'King Ferdinand would have been pleased if Aragon had rebelled so he might have an excuse to reconquer the province and impose his own laws.'

Philip had that very opportunity after crushing the Aragon Revolt (1591) but, although the justiciar could in future be dismissed at will and foreigners appointed, he adopted a moderate policy and preserved many fueros. However, it would be hard to accept Henry Kamen's comment, in *Spain 1469–1714: A Society of Conflict* (1983), that 'The advance of local autonomy in his reign led to an increase in liberty.'

The Council of Italy oversaw the Castilian viceroy of Naples. Naples sent grain to mainland Spain, on which the population depended due to their own infertile soil. Food riots caused a revolt in Naples (1585), crushed by Spanish troops with heavy reprisals. Blocked by powerful nobles, factional feuds and the local parliament, Philip failed to reform Sicily's legal system. Milan was a vital link in Spanish supply routes when the Ottoman Turks were pressing westwards. 'We cannot trust Italy to the Italians', Don Luis de Requesens, governor of Milan, wrote arrogantly, 'although they are not Indians, they have to be treated as such.'

The far-flung nature of the Americas made unworkable any attempt to centralise control. Geoffrey Parker, in *The Grand Strategy of Philip II* (1998), calculates that post from Mexico and Peru could take four to nine months, while from the Philippines it could take two years. The Council of the Indies, comprising professional lawyers, often ignorant of the Americas, monitored viceroys in Mexico and Peru, who were bombarded with royal edicts and regulations. They had to refer disputes to appeal courts staffed by lesser aristocrats, who spied on them and checked their innovations. From 1565, each large Indian town had a *corregidor de Indios* to collect taxes and control native workers. Indians were kept docile by the belief that royal government would protect them. However, Philip's authority in the New World existed only on paper.

How far was Philip II's power limited by an obsession with paperwork?

'Administrative chaos' or El Prudente?

Philip was known as a 'Paper King' as early as the 1550s. Garrett Mattingly, in *The Armada* (1959), calls Philip II 'the chief clerk of the Spanish empire'. Helmut Koenigsberger, in 'The Statecraft of Philip II' in *The European Studies Review, 1* (1971), sees:

> The lonely King in his small work-room in the Escorial, poring over reports and maps, annotating minutes in his all but illegible, loopy handwriting, itself almost a visual image of the circles of command and power endlessly returning back to the writer.

Philip demanded accurate, regularly-revised reports on council matters, and scrawled corrections and comments in tired, untidy writing. Only for six months in the whole reign was Spain at peace, causing bundles of papers from the Council of War to expand tenfold. He signed hundreds of memoranda a day and referred to 'those devils, my papers'.

Philip's insistence on written information, his refusal to attend council meetings and listen to spoken arguments, his slow decision-making and his time-wasting interest in trivia weakened government. A. W. Lovett, in *Early Habsburg Spain* (1986), agrees. He writes:

> Perhaps he hoped that application and annotation would serve for insight and resolution, the two qualities he most obviously lacked.

But, Henry Kamen, in *Philip of Spain* (1997), claims, 'Details were

An internal memorandum ('billete') of the Spanish government. 'Billetes' had wide margins so the King could add his comments. Here, Philip is replying (left) to the itinerary prepared by Don Juan de Idiaquez (right) for the voyage of the Armada from Lisbon to the Channel. Idiaquez had used a range of maps and a ship's Rutter (log). Philip replies at length that he too checked two further maps and the Rutter himself, and found a mistake in the spelling of a place name.

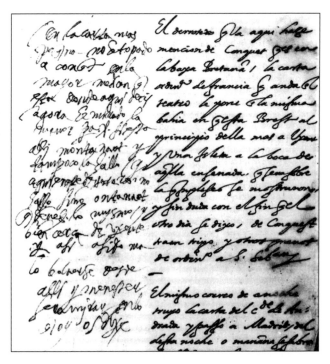

never indulged in to the detriment of his overall strategy.' Geoffrey Parker, in *The Grand Strategy of Philip II* (1998), likens Philip's governmental style to a 'panopticon' in which only the person at the centre can see everything. Yet Philip admitted that he found some reports incomprehensible, despite reading them several times. The King's 'limited intelligence, suspicion and spying on his ministers' caused 'administrative chaos', writes Helmut Koenigsberger, and 'at times an almost complete breakdown of government'.

Philip's desk became muddled and urgent papers were mislaid, as he was always on the move from one palace to another. He suffered from migraines and had to wear spectacles after 1580, although never in public. Engulfed in a sea of paperwork, he expanded the system of select **juntas**, which had featured in his government since the 1540s.

Juntas: committees containing specialists in the issue under discussion.

Even when he had all the information, and he never felt he had it *all*, he was reluctant to make a decision. Gonzalo Perez said, 'Decisions are taken so slowly that even a cripple could keep up with them,' and Pope Pius V commented, 'Your Majesty spends so long considering your undertakings that, when the time to perform them comes, the occasion has passed.' Yet A. W. Lovett, in *Early Habsburg Spain* (1986), called indecision 'an instrument of statecraft', and Geoffrey Parker called it a 'wait-and-see' mentality used also by

Elizabeth I, quoting Philip's own words: 'He who rushes matters in difficult circumstances, loses credibility (*reputación*).'

Roger Merriman, in *The Rise of the Spanish Empire in the Old World and the New: Vol IV The Prudent King* (1934) interprets 'El Prudente', as the 'cautious' King. However, Jaime Vicens Vives, in *Approaches to the History of Spain* (1967) translates the Castilian 'prudente' as 'basing decisions on reason alone, without emotion', suggesting 'wisdom' rather than 'caution'. Philip frequently changed his mind while reaching a decision, leading his detractors to accuse him of double-dealing. Gonzalo Perez explained:

> 'His Majesty makes and will make mistakes, because he discusses matters with several people, now with one then with another, hiding something from one but revealing it to others.'

Was Philip II's a strong or weak autocracy?

Generally historians accept the view of Jaime Vicens Vives, in *The Administrative Structure of the State in the Sixteenth and Seventeenth Centuries* (1971), that Philip aimed for 'maximum concentration of power at the apex and minimum diffusion of that power downward'. Philip was in sole charge, dutifully obeying his father's advice: 'Transact business with many and do not bind yourself to, or become dependant upon, any individual.' However, Geoffrey Parker, in *The World is Not Enough: The Imperial Vision of Philip II of Spain* (2001), argues that his desire to please God gave him a deep concern for public opinion and his role in history, so he often consulted confessors on the effects of his actions. Fray Diego de Chaves (confessor 1578–92) once threatened, 'God obliges me to deny Your Majesty all sacraments unless you do what I say.' Philip dutifully obliged.

Letrados: university-trained lawyers of humble origin.

Although councils were staffed by **letrados**, noble influence and patronage undermined Philip II's autocracy. The early influence of Ruy Gomez, Prince of Eboli, led to his nickname 'rey' (king) Gomez, but Philip chose the Duke of Alva's solution to the Netherlands problem (1566) over Eboli's. Historians conclude that he deliberately encouraged feuds among his officials in order to 'divide and rule'. However, Henry Kamen, in *Philip of Spain* (1997), claims Philip 'allowed differences of opinion and advice, which could help rather than hinder efficiency'. Kamen praises Philip for keeping the factions in balance, and maintaining their unquestioned loyalty to him, despite confusion. After the removal of Antonio Perez in 1579, afraid of appearing weak, Philip took a firm stand against factionalism.

Segovia Woods letters: in February 1565, Count Egmont arrived in Madrid to negotiate Philip's relaxation of the Netherlands heresy laws. Egmont returned to Brussels early in April, mistakenly thinking he had won concessions from Philip. Philip's letters, signed at his country house in the Segovia Woods on 17 and 20 October 1565, finally arrived in Brussels between 16 November and 20 December 1565. The letters insisted on strict enforcement of the heresy laws, and provoked the first Netherlands Revolt.

Micromanage: personal control of every executive detail of policy.

Massacre of the garrison of Haarlem: one of several of Alva's massacres of town garrisons (companies of troops). The town was persuaded to surrender unconditionally, after a seven-month siege costing Philip two million ducats, and placed itself at the Spaniards' mercy. Alva ordered the execution of the 2000-strong garrison in cold blood.

Philip listened to the views of many ministers before finally adopting a policy for the Netherlands, yet shifted from a military solution to conciliation according to his financial strength. The Spanish Road entailed a hazardous four months journey to the Netherlands and, although Philip's postal system was among the most efficient in Europe, orders were usually out of date by the time they arrived. The **Segovia Woods letters**, and the despatch of the Duke of Alva's army, were pivotal decisions so affected. In *The Grand Strategy of Philip II* (1998), Geoffrey Parker blames Philip's desire to **micromanage** for causing policy swings when army commanders and governors on the spot lost face, and took matters into their own hands, making crisis decisions. In the cases of Alva's executions, and the **massacre of the garrison of Haarlem** after the town placed itself at his mercy, Philip accepted events as the unforeseen will of God, but mostly he deliberately prevented Alva or Parma pursuing what, to them, seemed the wisest policy. Although his commanders advised him it might end the conflict, the King forbade the cutting of the dykes to flood the provinces (1574), fearing the Netherlands would never accept conquest on these terms and not wishing to contravene God's will or gain a reputation for cruelty.

Geoffrey Parker, in *The Grand Strategy of Philip II* (1998), comments that Philip 'instilled instant respect in all who met him', but Gregorio Marañón, in *Antonio Perez* (1963), accepts Perez's boast that Philip 'did nothing but approve decisions already made', and judges the King as irresolute and timid. Geoffrey Parker insists that Philip was firmly in charge and Henry Kamen asserts that Perez received no special royal favours. Councils never initiated policy but Parker accepts that 'council secretaries possessed great power', meeting ambassadors and highlighting urgent issues for the King's attention. As president of the Council of State and Inquisitor-General, Espinosa attended a variety of juntas that kept him almost as informed as the King, and died of 'mortification' when the King dismissed him. Philip later balanced two or more ministers whenever possible, for example Juan de Idiaquez, Cristóbal de Moura and the Count of Chinchon, to prevent any of them gaining too much power.

Mateo Vazquez was appointed royal secretary (1572–85) and not until 1594 did Philip allow his son, later Philip III, to sign orders, then commenting, 'God, who has given me so many kingdoms, has denied me a son capable of ruling them.' Towards the end of Philip II's reign, a critic described Philip's as 'the largest brain in the world'. Yet, his authoritarian stubbornness undermined effective government. Although he freely admitted that he would not 'break his brains' trying to understand financial affairs, he refused to allow Juan de Ovando to reform the financial system in 1574; instead declaring bankruptcy for a third time. Days after the King's death, Don Martin de Padilla, the commander of the Spanish High Seas fleet, complained:

> 'Men will see what the Spaniards are worth, now that they have a free hand and are no longer subject to a single brain that thought it knew all that could be known, and treated everyone else as a blockhead.'

Historians portray Philip's character as a mixture of strengths and weaknesses. He dutifully obeyed his father's *Instructions*, but remembered Charles' weakness in abdicating. Geoffrey Parker, in *Philip II* (1979), portrays a high-minded autocrat of rigid principle with supreme power, obsessively afraid of appearing weak. In *The Grand Strategy of Philip II* (1998), Geoffrey Parker adds:

> [Philip II] was simply at a loss, when the course dictated by principle seemed impossible, as in the case of the Dutch Revolt, or when his principles broke down, as in the case of Escobedo and Perez.

Henry Kamen goes further, seeing him as a weak agent within a strong structure. He concludes:

> Philip was never at any time in adequate control of events, or of his kingdoms, or even of his own destiny. He could do little more than play the dice available to him.

Was Philip II a cruel tyrant or a 'Paper King'?

1. Read the following extract and answer the question.

   > *'That the centre of the web lay in Spain bred many consequences, one of which was the growth of a sedentary administration. The other parts of the empire slipped into the role of satellites and Castile into that of the metropolitan power.'*

   > (F. Braudel, *The Mediterranean and the Mediterranean World in the Age of Philip II*, HarperCollins, 1972.)

   Using the information in the extract above, and from this section, evaluate how far Philip II centralised his power over Spain and its empire.

2. How far was Philip II himself to blame for his problems in administering his lands?

2 Did Philip II strengthen the Catholic Church?

To what extent did he enforce the decrees of the Council of Trent?

To what extent did the Inquisition strengthen the Spanish Church?

How far was he the champion of the Counter-Reformation?

Framework of events

1557–62	Inquisitors discover 'Protestants' in Valladolid, Burgos, Salamanca and Seville
1558	Inquisitor General Fernando de Valdés arrests Bartolomé de Carranza, Archbishop of Toledo, for heresy
1559	Inquisitor-General Fernando de Valdés issues First Index of 670 prohibited texts
1560–9	Granada Inquisition active: 88 per cent of victims Moriscos
1562/3	Final session of Council of Trent issues decrees to reaffirm orthodox Catholic doctrine and to discipline the clergy; 100 Spanish clergy present
1563	Publication of the Tridentine decrees in Spain
1566	Outbreak of Netherlands Revolt against Philip's rule (until 1609)
1567	Philip II releases Carranza for trial in Rome
1568–70	Moriscos Revolt against Philip's rule and their subsequent dispersal throughout Spain
1571	Battle of Lepanto
1572	Philip creates new archdiocese of Burgos
1578	Philip signs truce with Ottoman Turks
1583/4	Inquisitor-General Quiroga issues Second Index of 3500 prohibited (1583) and expurgated (1584) texts

WHILE Protestantism diversified, the Catholic Church entered a period of consolidation after the Council of Trent (1545–63). Historians agree that Philip saw himself as champion of the Catholic faith: God's chosen instrument in stemming the tide of militant international Calvinism for the Counter-Reformation. His inherited title of 'Catholic King' bound his 'messianic vision' to that of Rome, but a Catholic united front was undermined by the isolation of the Spanish national Church and Philip's clashes with the papacy.

To what extent did Philip II enforce the decrees of the Council of Trent?

What was Philip II's religious inheritance?

Philip inherited the titles of 'Catholic King' and 'King of Jerusalem', first granted by Spanish Pope Alexander VI to his great-grandfather, Ferdinand of Aragon, conqueror of the **Moors** (1492) and combatant in the Italian Wars (1494–1559). He also inherited control of Church revenue and appointments, and a national Inquisition (1478), although popes regretted this loss of power. Spanish monarchs ignored papal bulls and protests, and prohibited **appeals to Rome**. As a result, the Spanish Church was traditionally seen as militant, exclusive and orthodox, and policed by a state Inquisition.

Charles V, as **Holy Roman Emperor**, had a duty to defend Catholicism from heresy, which he attempted by proposing the General Church Council, which met at Trent (1545–63), and by fighting Protestant princes when his other commitments allowed him. The Imperial title and Austrian lands passed to Philip's uncle, Ferdinand, followed by his son Maximilian II, who was Philip's cousin and father-in-law. After the **Peace of Augsburg** (1555), the Austrian Habsburgs turned their attention to the Ottoman threat in Eastern Europe, and Philip, as 'Catholic King', took on the global role of 'champion of Catholicism'.

Historians have argued that the reason Protestant heresy did not touch Spain, was the resilience of Spanish Catholicism after the reforms of Ximénes de Cisneros, Archbishop of Toledo (1495–1517). However, his purge of clerical abuses had lost its effect by 1556 and Church wealth was unevenly distributed, resulting in a generally uneducated and corrupt clergy. Cisneros' foundation of the University of Alcalá in 1499 stimulated humanist thought, stifled by the Inquisition after the Protestant schism (1529). During this period of toleration, a tradition of Spanish mysticism fused with humanism to stimulate spiritual revival in the Spanish Church and in the broader Catholic Reformation.

Philip's personal piety was unquestioned: the Escorial was a monastery, his bed in the royal apartment in view of the High Altar of its church; he heard mass daily; he attended communion four times a year, and went into retreat at a monastery each Holy Week.

Moors: Muslim, black North-African race, which ruled much of Spain during the Middle Ages. Finally conquered in 1492.

Appeals to Rome: applications for reconsideration, by the Pope, of a court judgement made by the Spanish Inquisition or Church.

Holy Roman Emperor: the political, crusading arm of the papacy, an elective title, giving the holder figurehead rule over the states of Germany, Austria and Bohemia. The Habsburg family were also hereditary rulers of Austria.

Peace of Augsburg: an agreement (1555) signed by Charles V's brother Ferdinand, on Charles' behalf, with the princes of the Holy Roman Empire, allowing each German prince to choose the official state religion of his province, either Catholic or Lutheran (with the exception of Archbishop Electors, who had to stay Catholic). Subjects were forced to conform or go into exile.

Henry Kamen, in *Philip of Spain* (1997), denies that Philip was a religious fanatic, citing his letters to his daughters which contained no reference to religion, but admits that in old age Philip became more obsessed with religion, quoting Philip's statement of 1590: 'The cause of religion has been and is my principal guide in everything I have done and do.' Geoffrey Parker, in *The World is Not Enough: The Imperial Vision of Philip II of Spain* (2001) calls Philip's attitude 'messianic imperialism', comprising three elements: the belief that God had chosen him to rule expressly to achieve His purpose in the world; that God held him under special protection; and that, if necessary, God would intervene directly to help him succeed. In 1856, Motley observed, 'He considered himself, not a king, but a god.'

Did the Council of Trent 'revolutionise' the Spanish Church?

'There is no Pope in Spain,' contemporaries declared, as papal concessions had made the Spanish Church a department of state. John Lynch observes, in *Spain Under the Habsburgs: Empire and Absolutism 1516–1598* (1964), that the crown's control over the Church 'was probably more complete in Spain in the 16th century than in any other part of Europe, including Protestant countries with an **Erastian** system'. Philip was aware, however, that Rome's priority in calling the Council of Trent was to reassert papal supremacy.

Erastian: state sovereignty over the Church.

Henry Kamen, in *Spain 1469–1714: A Society of Conflict* (1983), argues that the Council of Trent 'revolutionised Spanish Catholicism'. Philip's deep respect for his father, who had proposed the Council, explains his personal reform proposals and the one hundred or more high-quality Spanish envoys he sent to its third session (1562). Catholic revival was embodied in the **Tridentine decrees** on doctrine and discipline. Although Philip formally accepted the decrees two weeks after their issue by the Pope (1563), he instructed his lawyers to ensure that they contained nothing to infringe his powers or those of the Inquisition, before beginning an ambitious modernisation programme for the national Spanish Church. Obsessively supervising all reforms in his dual role as *rex et sacerdos* (king and priest), Philip II convened provincial councils to establish a strict moral code to remove corruption.

Tridentine decrees: Church regulations on doctrine and discipline, which reaffirmed papal power, the Latin Vulgate Bible, celibacy of the priesthood, and entrusted bishops to ensure the clergy were educated, moral and hardworking.

Conventuals: Franciscan monks with permission to relax their vow of poverty.

Regular clergy: traditionally directly controlled from Rome, in international organisations, for example Franciscans, Augustinians and Dominicans.

Historians have agreed on the effectiveness of Philip's dissolution of decayed monasteries and **Conventuals**. This strengthened and spiritually revived the **regular clergy**, who carried out important

Secular clergy: priests, bishops, archbishops.

Seminaries: Church-funded schools.

missionary work in rural areas. To strengthen the authority of the **secular clergy**, Philip created an archbishop of Burgos (1572), a bishop of Valladolid and six bishops in Aragon. Geoffrey Parker, in *The World is Not Enough: The Imperial Vision of Philip II* (2001), argues that Philip personally assisted bishops in setting up **seminaries** and harassed those who would not do so. Clergy were educated to preach, hear confessions and teach Sunday schools, while visitations regularly checked their vestments, celibacy and church records. Philip abolished the old Mass, with his own contribution to the new text, and issued a new prayer book and calendar. However, rural Spaniards were backward and semi-pagan, with little understanding of doctrine or liturgy.

Philip decorated his churches and palaces with religious art, which was a visual aid for the illiterate in grasping a message Northern European Protestants proselytised through the Word. Philip's favourite painting was by his bedside, Hieronymus Bosch's *Garden of Earthly Delights*, with its vivid and surreal reminder of the sinner's fate. The Escorial itself stood as a granite bastion against heresy, a symbol of the power and strength of the Catholic faith.

The Garden of Earthly Delights (1500) comprises a central panel depicting lust, a left panel devoted to Adam and Eve, and a right panel portraying the gruesome punishments inflicted on the sinner in Hell. In this central panel, Bosch uses surreal images to evoke the transient nature of pleasure based on lust. 'Happiness is like a glass and soon breaks', ran an ancient Flemish proverb, so Bosch depicts lovers, rapt, inside a bubble that shuts out reality.

The effectiveness of reform depended on the quality of the local bishop, but clerical wages were low and ignorance and superstition were rife in the Spanish clergy, who often refused to apply the changes. Efforts to centralise the practice of local religion on the parish, and formalise it, failed to eradicate festivals and ceremonies that gave colour, drama and entertainment to the people's expression of their faith. William Christian, in *Local Religion in Sixteenth-Century Spain* (1981), draws attention to superstitious practices remaining in outlying areas, such as immersing a saint's image in the river to bring rain. Helen Rawlings, in *Church, Religion and Society in Early Modern Spain* (2002), suggests that divisions of authority between lay and church patrons at local level also made reform inconsistent, while inaccessibility obstructed the missions to remote, countryside areas, where there were often no priests. She concludes that 'Spanish Catholicism retained its diverse and popular roots.'

Index: list of prohibited, censored or expurgated texts, usually banned by the authorities because they were considered deviant from established orthodoxy but, in some cases, they were texts merely disliked by the Inquisitor-General.

While shrines of local saints remained and superstitious practices continued, it was no wonder magic was high on the list of proscribed topics for the **Index**, yet there were 200 books on magic in Philip's library. Geoffrey Woodward, in *Philip II* (1992), concludes, 'The condition of the Spanish Church appears to have been largely unreformed at the end of the century,' as Philip's own relic collection bears witness.

To what extent did the Inquisition strengthen the Spanish Church?

What was the role of the Spanish Inquisition?

Philip's reputation abroad owed less to reform and more to the terrors of the Inquisition. The printing presses of Heidelberg, Geneva and the Netherlands, well versed in propaganda for God's Calvinist elect, linked the Inquisition with persecution of heretics, although few had penetrated Spain. Persuaded by the Black Legend, John Motley, in *The Rise of the Dutch Republic* (1856), sees the Spanish Inquisition as:

Familiars: non-clerical officials of the Inquisition.

[A] bench of monks without appeal, having its **familiars** in every house, diving into the secrets of every fireside, judging and executing its horrible decrees and practising torture without responsibility.

Henry Kamen, in *The Spanish Inquisition: A Historical Revision* (1997) (see **Landmark Study**, opposite), reveals Inquisitors to have

Landmark Study **The book that changed people's views**

H. Kamen, ***The Spanish Inquisition: A Historical Revision*** (Weidenfeld & Nicolson, 1997)

This study revises Kamen's earlier works on the Inquisition and society in Spain, in response to Benzion Netanyahu's *The Origins of the Inquisition* (1995). Kamen uses newly-available sources to transform views on the Spanish Inquisition, setting it into the context of Spain's social and cultural structures. He dispels, as myths, its intolerance of racial minorities and its use of torture and burning. Kamen claims that the Inquisition's strict use of censorship, with which it had traditionally been accredited, was ineffective and its place in everyday life marginal. Kamen portrays the institution as an inefficient state bureaucracy, seeking to fulfil its educative and moral role, as well as its official religious function, within a society of conflict and racial tensions. Together with his other studies, he does more than any other historian to enhance the image of Philip II and his reign. Some historians feel that he goes too far in expurgating the Black Legend.

Autos de fe: literally 'acts of faith' — public ceremonies of humiliation for those accused and imprisoned by the Inquisition for heresy, and burning at the stake for the guilty and unrepentant.

been 'an elite state bureaucracy' of trained lawyers, often laymen with the same background as councillors of state, corregidors and high court lawyers, rather than small-minded clerics or dedicated, fanatical heresy hunters. Inquisitors had no knowledge of heretic ideas, causing a wave of hysteria to greet the discovery of enclaves of 'Lutherans' (some were harmless mystics) in the areas of Valladolid, Burgos, Salamanca and Seville (1557–62). Historians have expressed scepticism at the timing of these revelations, suspecting Inquisitorial self-interest to impress the new monarch and hasten his return to Spain from the Netherlands. Philip himself attended the **autos de fe**, but did not stay to see the burnings – 77 in all. Henry Kamen estimates that only 7 per cent of those accused between 1540 and 1614 were Protestants, mainly foreigners, and less than half a dozen were burnt for Protestantism in Spain after 1562. In 1565, concerned about laxity, Philip wrote:

> Let all prisoners be put to death, and suffer them no longer to escape through neglect, weakness and bad faith of the judges. If any are too timid to execute the edicts, I will replace them by men who have more heart and zeal.

Henry Kamen, in *The Spanish Inquisition: A Historical Revision* (1997), argues that prisoners often asked to be transferred to the Inquisition's jails as conditions were better there than in state prisons; its officials used torture in only 10 per cent of cases and acquitted 2 per cent of those accused. Although 40 000 people came before the Inquisition, fewer than 250 were burned at the stake during the 42-year reign. The Spanish Inquisition also denied the existence of 'witchcraft', while late 16th-century 'scientific' estimates suggest there were 1.8 million witches in Europe.

Auto de fe at which those tried by the Inquisition had their sentences pronounced, after being paraded before the public who came to watch their humiliation, usually in the central square of a major town. The occasions were used to edify good Catholics, and inspire with terror those wavering in their faith.

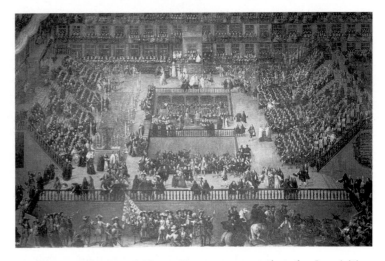

Suprema: Council of the Inquisition in Madrid.

Helen Rawlings and Henry Kamen suggest that the Inquisition was ineffective, unlike the Dutch image of an all-powerful terror machine, repeated by John Motley, in *The Rise of the Dutch Republic* (1856). The **Suprema**, and its Inquisitor-General in Madrid, oversaw 15 tribunals with 45 Inquisitors throughout a Spanish population of eight million.

However, many historians still agree with Geoffrey Woodward's suggestion, in *Philip II* (1992), that the Inquisition was 'an instrument of terror, directing an apparatus of social and political control'. Inquisition tribunals often encroached on state jurisdictions, imposing imprisonment without trial and flogging in cases concerning their own officials. Measures endorsed by the Cortes failed to prevent this, producing clashes between tribunals and civil authorities. But Kamen, in *The Spanish Inquisition: A Historical Revision* (1997), argues that Philip never wished to extend it to the Netherlands, despite Dutch propaganda, and claims the Inquisition 'rarely took any action that was nakedly political, so it would be mistaken to regard it as an instrument of state'. The cases of **Carranza** and Perez might suggest otherwise. Henry Kamen claims that its

Bartolomé Carranza, Archbishop of Toledo (1503–76)
A Dominican, educated at Alcalá and Salamanca Universities, he taught theology at Valladolid, was censor of the Inquisition and attended the Council of Trent. Philip II appointed him Archbishop of Toledo, primate of the Spanish Church, but in 1558 Inquisitor-General Valdés had him arrested for heresy. Pope Pius V ordered him to Rome for trial, initiating a nine-year struggle between the Spanish Inquisition and the papacy, only resolved when Philip released Carranza for trial in Rome (1567) by the new Pope Gregory XIII, rather than lose the right to collect the cruzada tax. After a further nine-year trial, Carranza was found not guilty, but died soon afterwards.

impact on the daily lives of Spaniards was infrequent and marginal. He argues that Inquisitors in towns dealt with a large number of accusations by neighbours, concerning sex outside marriage, swearing and blasphemy, whereas people in the countryside were lucky if they ever saw an Inquisitor in their entire lives. Kamen also refutes the generally-held claim that the Inquisition stifled Spain's cultural development and so weakened the Church. He describes as myth the view that Spaniards 'had to guard their speech carefully' and 'the image of a nation sunk in inertia and superstition because of the Inquisition'. Helen Rawlings, in *Church, Religion and Society in Early Modern Spain* (2002), disagrees, arguing that the Inquisition sought to control the speech, thoughts and behaviour of all Spaniards, making everyone watch their words carefully and those of their neighbour. In 1559, the import of foreign books was banned and the Council of Castile was empowered to license all literature. The 1559 Spanish Index of 670 prohibited books had grown by five times in its second edition (1583/4). Many of the titles were by authors disliked by the Inquisitor-General, who wished to shape literary taste. Some publications were **expurgated** to prevent their censorship, while many banned titles were deposited in the Escorial library for safekeeping. The effectiveness of censorship is now generally disputed by historians, because Spanish printing was the worst in Europe and Spaniards actually printed more books abroad during the last decades of Philip's reign than they had ever done before. While Kamen accepts that 'Spain had always been, and remained, an isolated backwater out of touch with the mainstream of European cultural development,' he argues that this was no fault of the Inquisition.

Expurgated: amended by removing offensive sections.

More recently, historians have emphasised the educative role of the Inquisition, especially in rural areas. Henry Kamen, in *The Spanish Inquisition: A Historical Revision* (1997), and Helen Rawlings, in 'The New History of the Spanish Inquisition' in *The Historian* (1997), comment on an impressive rise in literacy in some areas, as uneducated peasants learned the Lord's Prayer, for example, to avoid falling foul of the Inquisitors' questions. Jean-Pierre Dedieu, in 'Christianisation in New Castile' in *Culture and Control in Counter-Reformation Spain* (1992), calls the Inquisition a 'gigantic teaching-machine'. Helen Rawlings agrees, although she suggests that holy brotherhoods were just as significant as the Church and Inquisition in strengthening educational and moral standards.

Convivencia: coexistence of Catholics, Jews and Moors until the reign of Ferdinand and Isabella.

Philip inherited a suspicious and divided society in Spain, after the destruction of *convivencia* by his great-grandparents, who 'created within a united Spain a society of conflict', argues Henry

Conversos: Spanish Jews forcibly converted to Catholicism. Some conversos were secret Judaisers.

Kamen, in *Spain 1469–1714: A Society of Conflict* (1983). Ferdinand had seen secret Judaism everywhere, and encouraged their neighbours to denounce **conversos**, to strengthen the Church. In *The Spanish Inquisition: A Historical Revision* (1997), Henry Kamen argues that Philip adopted a more enlightened policy, appointing to office known conversos and refusing to extend 'purity' laws or strictly enforce existing ones.

The Revolt of the Moriscos (1568–70) is generally seen as evidence of Philip's repression of unorthodox racial minorities under the inherited 'purity of the blood' policy. Although Moriscos accounted for 88 per cent of those condemned by the Inquisition of Granada (1560–9), there were few Inquisitorial familiars in the Morisco towns where they were really needed. After their two-year revolt, the King shrank from expelling Moriscos, although exile of non-conformists was established practice by German princes seeking state orthodoxy under the Peace of Augsburg (1555). Helen Rawlings, in *Church, Religion and Society in Early Modern Spain* (2002), concludes that elements of Jewish and Moorish practice survived and were tolerated within the Church, weakening its orthodoxy.

Did Philip II support Catholic Orders in strengthening the Church?

Discalced Carmelite Order: a new branch of the Carmelite order ('discalced' means 'without shoes'), which adopted a very strict, ascetic life, suffering hardship and silence. The male branch was founded by John of the Cross, and the female branch by St Teresa of Avila.

By the time of Philip's accession, mystics, such as Teresa of Avila and John of the Cross, had to protect themselves by seeking powerful patrons. Teresa's patron was King Philip himself, shown by his recognition of the **Discalced Carmelite Order** (1562). Philip II's sister, Joanna, Regent of Spain during his absence (1554–9), was an enthusiastic follower of **Ignatius Loyola**, and corresponded with him secretly under the pseudonym of 'Mateo Sanchez'. She was secretly admitted to the all-male Society of Jesus in 1554, allowed to take her vows, and temporarily became the only female Jesuit in history. Philip's half-sister, Margaret of Parma, also pledged to 'further the interests' of the Jesuits in 1556, the year Loyola died.

Philip showed no special favour to the Jesuits, partly because of their fourth oath of obedience to the Pope and because of their intense rivalry with the Dominicans, who controlled the

| **Ignatius Loyola (1491–1556)** He was founder (first general) of the Society of Jesus, known as the Jesuit Order. He was a mystic, from a minor Basque | aristocrat family, and a charismatic ex-professional soldier, who was wounded at Pamplona (1521). He wrote *The Spiritual Exercises* – methodical prayers to enhance spiritual fitness, | and rules of the Jesuit Order. 6000 of his letters to missionaries worldwide are still in existence today in state, private or church archives. |

Inquisition. Loyola's *Spiritual Exercises* was included in the 1559 Index, for encouraging an interior form of religious experience. However, Philip encouraged their first wave of activity in the 1560s, and was rewarded with Jesuit support in his acquisition of Portugal. By the 1580s, however, he began to suspect General Aquaviva and other Italian generals of spying for a hostile papacy, but he failed to restrict Jesuit power and bring them under his control.

Geoffrey Scammell, in *The First Imperial Age: European Overseas Expansion C. 1400–1715* (1989), writes that the objective of the Jesuit New World mission was 'the creation of an Americas replica of the Apostolic Church', but he agrees with Helen Rawlings, *Church, Religion and Society in Early Modern Spain* (2002), that 'The initial euphoria generated by the prospect of establishing a utopian civilisation, soon gave way to pessimism and despair.' Henry Kamen, in *Spain's Road to Empire: The Making of a World Power, 1492–1763* (2003), suggests that Madrid failed to keep all missionary Orders under strict surveillance, and transfer Indians from their scattered communities to live in town parishes controlled by priests and bishops. Jesuits provided mission hospitals and schools, but failed to protect American Indians from the excesses of the colonists and of some missionaries themselves. Argument, persuasion and good example were applied in converting the Indians, but crude violence was used too, with, for example, the torture of over 4000 Yucatan Indians.

Reports of murder, even cannibalism, led missionaries to seek military support. Christian teachings conflicted with the native experience of exploitation, slavery, humiliation and oppression, producing confusion and misunderstanding. Sometimes missionaries used a vernacular Bible or native dictionaries and translators, some of them pictorial. As Indians were considered a subspecies of Christians, they were barred from the priesthood, and formed their own confraternities, such as that of the colonial saint, St Benedict the Moor. But, in 16th-century Mexico, argues Henry Kamen, in *The Spanish Inquisition: A Historical Revision* (1997), 95 per cent of the population never had contact with the Inquisition. The old and new faiths were practised as one, with the Catholic God just one among many local deities. Nakedness, polygamy, incest and human sacrifice were less openly practised and pagan religious organisation was destroyed. 'Churches were built on sites of pagan shrines, native dirges were incorporated into Latin chants, and colourful festivals were encouraged,' comments Geoffrey Scammell, in *The First Imperial Age: European Overseas Expansion C. 1400–1715* (1989), concluding, 'Conversion was often superficial and ephemeral.'

Kamen's research reveals publications by the missionary Orders in Madrid, registering successes in every corner of the empire, but with limitations. In the Portuguese empire (Spanish after 1580), administrators often obstructed non-Portuguese missionaries, while inhospitable terrain and climate, and strong native religions, further inhibited their work. Only in the Philippines did the Catholic faith make real inroads, thanks to the activities of Augustinian friars with the backing of colonial military force. Distance was again a major limitation, as shown by the example of the bishopric of Manila, which, as part of the archdiocese of New Spain in Mexico, was linked to Madrid via America.

In theory, Catholicisation of the American natives strengthened the Catholic Church by adding vast numbers of new believers in an eventual area 20 times the size of the Iberian Peninsula. But, in doing so, Catholic orthodox doctrine was weakened. It could be argued, however, that one of the strengths of revived Catholicism was that it welcomed pagans in order to educate and instruct them, in contrast to Calvinist rejection of them as **'reprobates'**.

Reprobates: Calvinists believed God predestined at birth His 'elect' for Heaven, and 'reprobates' for Hell.

How far was Philip II the champion of the Counter-Reformation?

Did Philip II's clashes with the papacy weaken the Catholic Church?

Philip's enemies portrayed him as a bigoted fanatic, cruelly suppressing God's elect, censoring His Word and using the terror of the Inquisition to increase his own power and that of the Roman Antichrist. Yet, shortly after Philip's accession, Pope Paul IV **excommunicated** him.

The King stubbornly supported the Inquisition, even when it brought him into open confrontation with Rome as in the case of Carranza, Archbishop of Toledo. In 1559, the Inquisition arrested Carranza for heresy in an attempt to set a precedent, to deny an archbishop the right to be tried by Rome. Carranza had earned the personal antagonism of Inquisitor-General Fernando de Valdés and Philip's scheming confessor Bernardo de Fresneda. Carranza remained under arrest in Spain until 1566, when Pius V was elected, and a threat to withhold the **cruzada tax** forced Philip to release him for trial in Rome. Carranza, although vindicated, died soon after. The Inquisition failed to strengthen its power, and for eight years, the Spanish Church was weakened by the absence of its Archbishop.

Excommunicated: officially excluded from communion with the Church. Pope Paul IV was a Neapolitan who resented Spain's rule of Naples and had a political axe to grind, so he allied with Philip's enemy, the French King. The excommunication ceased when the war ended.

Cruzada tax: royal grant of a papal subsidy, collected by right of Spain's crusades against the infidel.

Geoffrey Parker, in *The World is Not Enough: The Imperial Vision of Philip II of Spain* (2001), reveals Philip's interference in papal elections, even his resort to military and naval threats in the 1590s. He continually bullied popes to enforce his demands, actively dissuading Pius IV and Pius V from excommunicating Queen Elizabeth I in the 1560s, unable to take action against her at that time due to his other commitments. Mary Queen of Scots' links with Catholic France made her an unsuitable alternative to Elizabeth, even if the Church might be strengthened by her seizure of the English throne. When Pius V excommunicated Elizabeth without warning (1570), Philip continued to concentrate his efforts on the Turks, later angering Pope Gregory XIII (successor of Pius V) and provoking calls to end the cruzada, by signing a truce with the Turks in 1578.

Pope Sixtus V refused to pay the million ducats promised for the Armada, and Philip rebuked him in 1589 for ignoring the problem of Henry of Navarre, 'reminding him of the duties of the office of Pope'. As Spanish troops mobilised in Italy, it seemed that Philip's reign would end, as it had begun, with the Catholic King once more excommunicated, destroying the Catholic alliance. The death of Sixtus (1590) averted this, but Pope Clement VIII's recognition of Henry of Navarre's Catholicism (1593) left an unresolved Spanish rift with Rome at Philip's death.

Did Philip II's foreign policy strengthen the Catholic faith?

Sir Charles Oman, in *A History of the Art of War in the Sixteenth Century* (1937), epitomises the view of Black Legend historians by describing Philip as a 'systematic liar and hypocrite, who saw no means too low to secure his own autocratic power and triumph for the Roman Church'. If these ambitions clashed, which would be Philip's priority? Geoffrey Parker, in *The World is Not Enough: The Imperial Vision of Philip II* (2001), argues that Philip's consistent motivation was 'messianic vision'. However, some historians charge Philip with using Catholicism as a cloak for national and dynastic ambitions.

In 1566, Philip wrote to the Pope saying:

> Rather than suffer the least damage to religion and the service of God, I would lose all my states and a hundred lives if I had them; for I do not propose nor desire to be the ruler of heretics.

Although Philip may have been answering papal criticism of his personal absence from the Netherlands at a time of unrest, his words

Edict of Nantes:
1598 decree put into
effect by King Henry IV to
restore peace in France
after the Wars of Religion.
French Protestants were
given freedom of worship,
civil rights, royal subsidies
and 50 garrisons, 80 forts
and 150 other places of
refuge within the Catholic
French state — making
them 'a state within a
state'.

Peñón de Vélez: the
rocky outpost (Peñón) of
the port of Vélez on the
North-African coast.

William Allen: an
English Cardinal, exiled to
Flanders after Elizabeth's
Protestant Church
Settlement (1559), who
founded a College at
Douai, in Flanders, to train
seminary priests under the
protection of Philip II.

enhanced his reputation as 'Catholic King'. Henry Kamen, in *Philip of Spain* (1997), suggests Philip's denunciation of heresy was always in relation to rebellion. Philip's willingness, after 1591, to grant toleration in the Netherlands 'for a limited time', if the Dutch submitted to Spanish rule, might have been approved by Clement VIII who had accepted the **Edict of Nantes**.

Philip needed to impress the papacy in order to fund his foreign ventures. In 1564, he said 'The Pope is watching.' as he defended **Peñón de Vélez** from the Barbary corsairs; yet the victory benefited Spain more directly than the Catholic Church. He claimed the Battle of Lepanto (1571) as a Spanish triumph, in defence of Catholicism against militant Islam, yet his 1578 truce revealed that he was no crusader and Spanish national interests came first.

Fernand Braudel, in *The Mediterranean and the Mediterranean World in the Age of Philip II* (1949), writes that the Counter-Reformation 'turned the Spanish King into the champion of Catholicism, the defender of the faith' against heresy in the 1580s. R. A. Stradling, in *Europe and the Decline of Spain* (1981), argues that Philip was driven by *'reputaçión'* (spiritual self-esteem and prestige) and *'conservaçión'* (as God's custodian, preservation of his inheritance), but that both duties depended on his mission to uphold the Catholic Church. The Armada (1588) has been presented by some historians as primarily religious in intention, with **William Allen** ready to lead a revived English Catholic Church. Elizabeth I certainly feared that Philip's encouragement of English Catholics in plots such as that of Ridolfi (1571) and Throckmorton (1583) strengthened their resolve to oppose her. But, ultimately, the Armada merely wasted ten million ducats that might have been spent on recovering the Northern Netherlands for the Catholic Church.

Philip II united the Iberian Peninsula by completing the Habsburg strategy of 'matrimonial imperialism' and annexing Portugal (1580) in the name of the Church, preventing heresy spreading there. He retained the Southern Netherlands in the Catholic faith, vigorously revived due to missionary work and the drift of southern Calvinists to the north where Catholicism was officially outlawed. Yet Philip's rigid enforcement of the Netherlands heresy laws, and Alva's excesses, helped to make moderate Catholics into Calvinist rebels. From a positive viewpoint, Philip prevented the total loss of his Flemish inheritance, but viewed negatively, his 'messianic imperialism' was primarily responsible for the loss of valuable Catholic lands.

Some historians argue that Philip scored a major success in keeping France a Catholic country at a time when its monarchy might have become Calvinist. Whether the eventual conversion of Henry of Navarre in July 1593 can be credited to the intervention of Spanish forces after 1589, is a matter of conjecture. Philip himself did not see this as a triumph, as he continued to fight the French until bankruptcy and his final illness forced him to accept the Treaty of Vervins (1598). Historians generally interpret his actions as aggressive imperialism rather than defence of the faith. His own protestations to the Pope emphasised his mistrust of Henry's conversion, and only with hindsight can historians observe Henry's sincerity and his revival of French Catholicism. To Spain's detriment, France was to emerge as the strongest European power in the 17th century.

Philip both weakened and strengthened the Catholic Church. The Spanish Church was reformed under royal supervision, nationalised and purged of some of its corruption, but it retained the diversity of its belief and practice, despite the Inquisitorial drive towards exclusivity and orthodoxy. Spain both strengthened and weakened the reputation of the Church, with propaganda victories like Lepanto and Portugal, but with disasters like the Armada, the loss of the United Provinces, and its association with the Inquisition and the Black Legend. The Church gained a vast population of believers in Spain's global empire, at the expense of doctrinal orthodoxy. Above all, Philip's secretive character merely aroused suspicions that he put his own interests before God's, which he saw as one and the same.

Did Philip II strengthen the Catholic Church?

1. Read the following extract and answer the question.

   'The Inquisition was an instrument of terror directing a clandestine apparatus of social and political control and a very effective way of enforcing a code of religious instruction and moral ethics upon a largely uneducated and backward society.'

   (G. Woodward, *Philip II*, Longman, 1992.)

   Using the information in the extract above, and from this section, assess the effectiveness of the Spanish Inquisition under Philip II.

2. How far did Philip II's reforms revolutionise the Spanish Church?

Was Philip II's foreign policy 'Grand Strategy' or crisis management?

What motivated his foreign policy?

Was his policy aggressively imperialist after 1583?

Was his foreign policy defensive or religious up to 1580?

Did 'Grand Strategy' collapse in the 1590s?

Framework of events

1557	Philip's troops defeat French at Battle of St Quentin
	Philip declares bankruptcy
1559	Philip signs Treaty of Cateau-Cambrésis, ending Habsburg-Valois Wars
1560	Turks defeat Spanish invasion of island of Djerba
	Philip declares bankruptcy
1565	Philip's fleet relieves Turkish siege of Malta
1566	Outbreak of Netherlands Revolt against Philip's rule (until 1609)
	Death of Ottoman Sultan Suleiman the Magnificent
1567	Alva arrives in the Netherlands with 10 000 troops
1568	Outbreak of Moriscos Revolt against Philip's rule (until 1570)
1571	Holy League fleet destroys Ottoman navy at Battle of Lepanto
1573	Spain recovers Tunis and la Goletta
	Turks capture Cyprus
1574	Turks recapture Tunis and la Goletta
1575	Philip declares bankruptcy
1578	Philip signs truce with Ottoman Turks
1580	Philip acquires Portugal
1584	Death of Duke of Anjou
	Assassination of William of Orange
	Philip gives financial and military aid to French Catholic League in Treaty of Joinville
1585	English invade the Netherlands under terms of Treaty of Nonsuch
1588	Philip sends Spanish Armada to invade England
1590	Duke of Parma relieves Henry of Navarre's siege of Paris
1593	Henry of Navarre converts to Catholicism
1596	Philip at war against Triple Alliance (England, France, the United Provinces)
	Philip declares bankruptcy
1598	Philip makes peace with France at Treaty of Vervins

U NTIL the 1940s, Protestant historians repeated the claims of Spain's enemies: that Philip aggressively sought universal empire, driven by Counter-Reformation fanaticism. To Spanish historians, he embodied their national spirit in defence of the faith. They attributed debilitating war to his inheritance of the Netherlands.

Twentieth-century historians, seeking patterns of change, questioned whether Philip was aggressively imperialist or defensively nationalist. They agree that to defend sometimes necessitates attack, and discuss the motives behind his policy. Some historians question whether he had a policy at all, or whether he merely responded, pragmatically and inconsistently, to crises as they arose. Though Geoffrey Parker accepts that there was no 'blueprint for empire', he accepts that Philip followed a 'Grand Strategy'.

What motivated Philip II's foreign policy?

Religion

Since *Philip II* (1979), Geoffrey Parker has maintained that 'Religion was the mainspring of his foreign policy.' By 1998, in *The Grand Strategy of Philip II* (see **Landmark Study** see p. 46), Parker refined this as 'messianic imperialism': Philip's conviction that God would provide victory as long as he, in return, fulfilled his special obligation to God in defending the faith and conserving his lands. R. A. Stradling had argued a similar view in *Europe and the Decline of Spain* (1981), defining Philip's motivation:

- *Reputación*: the monarch's spiritual, perhaps psychological self-esteem, as well as his prestige in the eyes of Europe.

- *Conservación:* the preservation of the inheritance of which Philip was God's custodian.

Both duties depended on Philip's religious mission to maintain Catholic Christianity.

Reputation, Spanish prestige, personal interests

Philip himself declared in 1557 that the war against France was in defence of 'my states, as well as my honour and *reputación*, which I value above all else'. R. A. Stradling, in *Europe and the Decline of Spain* (1981), accepts that Philip's main aim in foreign policy was to protect Spanish prestige, and Geoffrey Woodward, in an article

Landmark Study   The book that changed people's views

G. Parker, *The Grand Strategy of Philip II* (Yale University Press, 1998)

Parker brings Philip II right up to date by drawing comparisons between his strategy and the 'Grand Strategy' of modern world superpowers. He sets out to explain Philip's strategic priorities in ruling the first global empire in history, to examine his decision-making processes and assess his constraints, both personal and external. Parker draws parallels with other absolute rulers in later centuries, and the management techniques used by 20th-century global empires. For example, Philip's refusal to flood the land during the Dutch Revolt has a parallel in President Lyndon Johnson's strategy in Vietnam. He concludes that Philip worked within strategy laid down by earlier Habsburg rulers, but added his own imperial vision as God's instrument, working in Iberian interests, drawing together a range of aims. He suggests that Philip was driven by 'messianic imperialism', similar to capitalist, communist or fundamentalist states today. Philip's success was frustrated by events, some of his own making, which tipped his priorities and pushed him into 'crisis management'. The existence of a 'Grand Strategy' is still widely questioned by scholars.

entitled 'Philip II's Foreign Policy: A Historical Controversy' in *History Review*, 21 (1995), argues, ' "Honour" and "reputation" counted for more than acquisition of new lands, fighting religious wars or creation of a universal monarchy.' Peter Pierson, too, in *Philip II of Spain* (1975), believes that Philip was 'motivated by personal obligations rather than by reasons of state'. Geoffrey Parker, in *The Grand Strategy of Philip II* (1998), argues that Philip's 'zero defects mentality' would not countenance failure, yet fail he did.

An alternative view: reactive rather than planned

Michele Suriano, Venetian ambassador to Spain, commented in 1559:

> 'The Emperor [Charles V] planned great designs but the King thinks less of increasing his own power than of obstructing the power of others.'

Fernand Braudel, in *The Mediterranean and the Mediterranean World in the Age of Philip II* (1949), argued, 'Never do we find general notions or grand strategies under Philip's pen.' Helmut Koenigsberger, in *Estates and Revolutions: Essays in Early Modern European History* (1971) accepts that Philip's ministers had 'no plan or programme for his reign' and Peter Pierson, in *Philip II of Spain* (1975), goes further, arguing:

> He had no universal plan for extending his power, or even the sway of the Church of Rome. He reacted, with varying degrees of decisiveness, only to particular situations rather than implementing some grand design.

Was there a 'policy' at all?

Peter Pierson, in *Philip II of Spain* (1975), states:

> [Philip's 'policy' was] a seemingly disjointed series of events with no unifying thread save for the universal consideration of cost, which from time to time forced Philip to reassess each course he was pursuing and give some one of them priority.

Pierson judges Philip as:

> ... diffident, rather demoralised, given to half measures and last-minute expedients. Like other contemporary rulers, timid, lacking energy, conservative, cautious, hesitant and parsimonious. As an instrument of God's will, his diffidence belied God's trust.

How does Parker reconcile 'crisis management' with 'Grand Strategy'?

The elements of 'Grand Strategy'

R. A. Stradling, in *Europe and the Decline of Spain* (1981), observes, 'The Spanish monarchy was already firmly committed to a pan-European political strategy.' This view is explored and developed by Geoffrey Parker, in *The Grand Strategy of Philip II* (1998). 'A global strategic vision clearly underlay initiatives undertaken by Philip's government,' he argues, as Philip inherited Habsburg imperial strategies, which had three main threads:

● *Matrimonial imperialism*: amalgamation of territories by dynastic inheritance.

● *Consolidation*: acquisition of territories adjacent to dynastic lands by purchase, negotiation or naked aggression.

● *No surrender*: no conquest should ever be returned.

Habsburg Holy Roman Emperors acted as the political arm of the papacy, and Philip obeyed his father's wishes in all matters. But he was the 'Catholic King', a Castilian, with an intense religious commitment typical of many of the Spanish aristocracy. The centre of gravity of Philip's inheritance had shifted; Spain was now at the heart of his Mediterranean empire, and Seville was the hub of New World trade. Geoffrey Parker argues that Philip added consistent strategies, personal to him:

● *Spanish national interest*: Iberia must take preference over all other lands.

- *Messianic imperialism*: defence of the Catholic Church, under the direct mandate of God, against enemies inside and outside Europe.

In the essay 'The Grand Strategy of Philip II and the Revolt of the Netherlands' in *The Origins and Development of the Dutch Revolt* (2001), Geoffrey Parker and González de León identify theoretical and practical principles that Philip followed – far from last-minute expedients.

Theoretical principles

- *Theological and ethical justification*: deep concern for his role in history and awareness of public opinion. Deep concern too for the ideological and propaganda effects of his actions.
- *Providentialism*: hope of God's protection and intervention, but provision for 'fortune' – unforeseen incidental reverses or God's punishment.
- *Reputation:* the King must strive at all costs to keep not only honour, but also all public appearances of honour.

Practical political and military principles

- *A defensive stance.*
- *The domino theory*: 'escalation of possible disasters' – if one territory were lost, the rest might follow.
- *The inevitability, even desirability of war*: to protect Spanish interests, but keeping war as far away from Iberia as possible.
- *A priority list*: Iberia and the Indies must take preference over all other lands, (Italy and the Mediterranean second, the Netherlands and Northern Europe third).
- *Dynastic solidarity*: solidarity with the Austrian Habsburgs, as long as this did not conflict with other policy principles.

Geoffrey Parker and González de León argue, 'A consistent direction for policy emerged from debate, even when principles conflicted.' They admit that the theory of a 'Grand Strategy' is far from accepted. John Lynch, in *Spain Under the Habsburgs: Empire and Absolutism 1516–1598* (1964), states, 'there was no order of priorities' in Philip's diverse concerns. Peter Pierson, in *Philip II of Spain* (1975), claims, 'The apparent disorder of the King's policies was not because of his clever dissimulation, but were as often the result of his confusion as his designs.'

Was Philip II's foreign policy defensive or religious up to 1580?

Was Philip II's foreign policy primarily defensive and conservative up to 1580?

Peter Pierson's claim, in *Philip II of Spain* (1975), that Philip's foreign policy was reactive, defensive and conservative, is supported by R. A. Stradling's view, in *Europe and the Decline of Spain* (1981), that Philip preserved his inheritance as God's custodian. Habsburg 'matrimonial imperialism' had secured for Philip control of Spain and the Netherlands, which would be strategically defended by Philip's marriage to Mary Tudor (1554). Her death, four years later, ended this potential consolidation of power, while bankruptcy, the death of his father and reports of heresy in Seville and Valladolid drew Philip home to the heart of his empire, Castile. At the Treaty of Cateau-Cambrésis (1559), he ended the Habsburg-Valois Wars (1494–1559), which had confirmed Habsburg control of Naples, Sicily and Milan. He fulfilled his aim of *'conservación'* by handing over to France only territories belonging to England, the Holy Roman Empire and Savoy. Michele Suriano, the Venetian ambassador, reported that Philip's aim 'was not to wage war so that he can add to his kingdoms, but to wage peace so that he can keep the lands he has'.

The far-flung nature of Philip's lands made keeping them a challenge. In the Mediterranean, trade rivalries, Barbary pirates and the naval strength of the advancing Ottoman Turks threatened the North-African outposts and the Spanish eastern coastline. Across the Atlantic, Spanish shipping came under attack from English and Dutch pirates eager to encroach upon Spain's monopoly of Caribbean and American trade. Heretics threatened the Low Countries, England, Scotland and France in what Philip saw as a concerted international attack on Catholicism. The acquisition of the Philippines (1565) and Portugal (1580) only served to aggravate his enemies' fears. R. A. Stradling, in *Europe and the Decline of Spain* (1981), concludes, 'It was inevitable that such an all-embracing political entity should be in a permanent condition of war.' There were only six months of complete peace in the entire 43-year reign. Geoffrey Parker, in *The Grand Strategy of Philip II* (1998), observes that Philip's Monarchy 'lacked geographical cohesion, so that several exposed parts repeatedly came under threat from one enemy or another'.

The papacy sought Spanish help to defend Italy's Adriatic coastline against Muslim raids. The French grasped every opportunity, even Muslim alliance, to break out of Habsburg encirclement. Strong forces were needed in the Netherlands to keep France in check, and the costs of warfare escalated. Luckily for Philip his opponents had their weaknesses: an inexperienced female ruler in England with a disputed succession; underage kings in France beset by civil war; defensive German princes fearful of Turkish proximity; and weak sultans and Persian distractions for the Ottomans, after the death of Sultan Suleiman the Magnificent (1566). Perhaps claims of Spain's Golden Age owed more to opponents' weaknesses than to Spanish strengths.

Charles advised his son in his *Instructions* to fulfil his dynastic obligations and conserve his inheritance by maintaining good relations with Portugal, England and Denmark. Philip obeyed by: marrying Mary Tudor; maintaining peace with England until 1585, despite years of irritating incidents; and annexing Portugal in 1580. To safeguard Spain's imports of Polish grain, Philip played Denmark off against Poland and Sweden in the Baltic, distracting them from helping the Dutch rebels. From 1567, advisers warned Philip of a 'domino theory' – if the Netherlands were lost, Spain's security and Philip's control of all his other lands would be in jeopardy. Defence of his Netherlands inheritance would lead to conflict with Protestant England in the 1560s, but his immediate priority was the Mediterranean.

Was Philip II the 'champion of Catholicism'?

Geoffrey Parker, in *The World is Not Enough: The Imperial Vision of Philip II of Spain* (2001), notes that Philip II, like Charles I and Oliver Cromwell a century later, believed in providentialism. Yet, Philip inherited a war with France's ally, the anti-Spanish Pope Paul IV, who promptly excommunicated him when a Spanish army threatened Rome. The haughty Castilian commander, the Duke of Alva, followed Philip's instructions to beg the Pope's mercy on bended knee when unconditional peace was agreed. Philip's leniency strengthened support in his Italian lands – showing that national interest coincided with religious duty. Leopold von Ranke, in *The Ottoman and the Spanish Empires in the Sixteenth and Seventeenth Centuries* (1843), observes:

> He came to regard the progress of his own power and the progress of religion as identical, and to behold the latter in the former.

R.A. Stradling, in *Europe and the Decline of Spain* (1981), considers Philip's 'prior and unquestioning task was to defend in arms the interests of God and His Church'. His title of 'Catholic King', inherited from his great-grandfather Ferdinand of Aragon, made him king and priest, obliged to defend the faith against heresy. As 'King of Jerusalem' – a title also inherited from Ferdinand – he was committed to defend Christendom from the infidel. He fought the Ottoman fleet at Djerba (1560) to defend Spain's North-African outposts, eastern coasts, trade and communications in the Western Mediterranean. Defeat cost him reputation, half his fleet and 10 000 Spanish prisoners, who were humiliatingly paraded through the streets of Istanbul. Financial weakness caused him to prioritise his many commitments. The refurbishment of his fleet generated a perennial drain on a Castilian economy already bankrupted twice in three years, suggesting that cost did not deter him from defending religion, empire and reputation.

Simultaneously, the Scottish Protestant rebellion produced Anglo-French confrontation and pleas from Rome and his brother-in-law Francis II for support against heresy. He had already agreed (March 1560) to defend Elizabeth I if she were attacked, fearing French influence if Mary Queen of Scots seized the English throne, so he actively *prevented* Pope Pius IV from excommunicating Elizabeth. Maintaining the status quo in Northern Europe, he pragmatically placed national interest before Catholicism, and Scotland was lost to the Presbyterian Lords of the Congregation. As France plunged into civil unrest, bringing militant heretics close to the Pyrenees, religion and the national interest united in one defensive strategy.

Defence of the crucial straits between Tunis and Sicily necessitated attack after the Ottoman assault on Oran (1563) and siege of Malta (1565). Philip restored *'reputación'* by the capture of Peñón de Vélez (1564) and relief of the siege of Malta (1565). The death of Ottoman Sultan Suleiman the Magnificent (September 1566), after 46 years of spectacular Ottoman advance, gave Philip a welcome respite. He seized the opportunity to crush the **iconoclastic** heretics in the Netherlands by despatching the Duke of Alva with 10 000 veteran troops. His motivation was stated in a letter to Pope Pius V (1566):

Iconoclastic: involving destruction of religious images.

> Rather than suffer the least damage to religion and the service of God, I would lose all my states and a hundred lives, if I had them; for I do not propose nor desire to be the ruler of heretics.

Although Geoffrey Parker, in *Philip II* (1979), accepts Philip's religious sincerity, he sees the letter as a reply to justified papal criticism of Philip's absence from the Netherlands when his presence might have avoided an 80-year war.

Tenth Penny tax: 10 per cent sales tax, raised to fund Alva's Spanish troops, but crippling for trade and commerce in the Netherlands, and extremely unpopular.

Cognitive rigidity: failure to improvise, reducing creativity in times of crisis; diminished receptivity to information that challenges existing beliefs; increased stereotyped thinking; and reduced tolerance for ambiguity, leading to premature termination of the search for information.

Philip, however, had far from extinguished the Ottomans, who captured Tunis and la Goletta and invaded the rich Venetian-held island of Cyprus (1570). Here was an opportunity for Philip to lead a religious crusade against the infidel and fulfil his inherited obligation as 'King of Jerusalem', but, unlike his father, he was no crusader. His reluctance to contribute troops suggests that defence of Rome, the Eastern Mediterranean and Venetian trade were not his priority, even if religion and *'reputación'* were. At the same time, the Duke of Alva was pleading for funds to maintain his army against Dutch hostility, but the parsimonious Philip fatally ordered the raising of the **Tenth Penny tax**, which largely contributed to the outbreak of the second Dutch Revolt (1572). Although Alva recognised 'the danger to the service of God and the King' in respect to 'domino theory', Philip prioritised defence of the Mediterranean. Geoffrey Parker, in *The Grand Strategy of Philip II* (1998), argues that 'micromanagement' and **'cognitive rigidity'** compounded his problems. Peter Pierson, in *Philip II of Spain* (1975), judges Philip's decisions as 'half measures and last-minute expedients' driven by shortage of money – in short, 'crisis management'.

Geoffrey Parker, in *The Grand Strategy of Philip II* (1998), explains the modern 'crisis management' model, as:

> A manager who tries to do everything in a dictatorial and secretive manner, who uses employees as simple functionaries, and when overwhelmed by such a burden of responsibility, restricts the goals of the organisation to the negative aim of coping with each successive challenge and trying to avoid mistakes.

He admits, 'This became the precise style of leadership adopted by Philip II at various critical junctures during his reign.' Parker's view of Philip as crisis manager seriously undermines his argument of a consistent 'Grand Strategy'.

Once Philip had agreed to support the Holy League in its naval campaign against the Ottomans, he openly admitted, 'Our *reputación* will certainly suffer if we do not provide what we promised.' Although Don John of Austria commanded the Christian fleet, and Philip claimed the Battle of Lepanto (1571) as a great Spanish victory, the majority of ships and troops were Venetian. Historians traditionally saw the battle as a pivotal event in the history of the Mediterranean, with the loss of 30 000 Turkish lives and 195 of 230 galleys of the previously invincible Turkish fleet. Cardinal Espinosa compared the event with the Biblical drowning of Pharaoh's army in the Red Sea, while Philip commissioned Titian's *painting Spain Coming to the Aid of Religion*, promoting his reputation as the champion of

The Holy League fleet, comprising the navies of Italy and Spain, commanded by Don John of Austria, defeated the Turkish navy off the coast of Greece at Lepanto, 1571.

Christendom. Philip's 'messianic vision' of God's favour was confirmed to him by the birth of a longed-for heir in the same year. Recent historians, however, agree with Peter Pierson that Lepanto was 'an empty victory'. The Turks went swiftly on to seize Cyprus, and although Don John captured Tunis and la Goletta (1573), the Turks rebuilt their fleet and later recaptured both (1574). Venice made a separate peace (1573), leaving Philip to shoulder the cost of the Mediterranean fleet, estimated at 60 000 ducats a month. Taken together with the soaring costs of the Dutch War and the waste of half a million ducats in an attempt to sweep the Channel of pirates, it is no wonder that Philip declared bankruptcy in 1575.

The Spanish 'King of Jerusalem' managed the crisis by cutting his losses. He extricated himself from the Mediterranean War by signing a truce with the Ottomans (1578) and a formal armistice (1580). The fury of Pope Gregory XIII was compounded by Philip's continued collection of the cruzada tax in Spain. But now Philip could resume the role of 'Catholic King' by sending funds and troops against the heretic rebels in the Netherlands. It is therefore debatable whether this does indeed show that Philip put national interest above religion. His 'messianic vision' was diverse, and he continued to view God's cause and his own as one. God's reward came when the throne of Portugal fell vacant, after the disappearance of his nephew King Sebastian, in Morocco (1578), and the death of his successor the elderly Cardinal Henry (1580). Habsburg 'matrimonial imperialism' now came to fruition.

The acquisition of Portugal 1580 – a 'tipping point'?

Geoffrey Parker, in *The Grand Strategy of Philip II* (1998), disagrees with Fernand Braudel's dismissal of the importance of 'events' in his 'total history' *The Mediterranean and the Mediterranean World in the Age of Philip II* (1949). Parker argues for the concept of 'the tipping point' – a small, perhaps military, event that begins a new trend in the linear course of history. The acquisition of Portugal turned Philip away from the Mediterranean to face, what Braudel calls 'that immense battlefield', the Atlantic.

Peter Pierson, in *Philip II of Spain* (1975), describes the unification of the Iberian Peninsula as 'the greatest triumph of his reign'. Philip himself remarked, 'I inherited, I bought, I conquered,' celebrating his entry to Lisbon, where he lived until 1583, trimming his beard and dressing in the Portuguese style. By defeating his rival **Dom Antonio**, he prevented heretics threatening Spain and Catholicism 'by the back door'. Spain gained 250 000–300 000 tons of shipping and a commercial empire stretching from Brazil to Goa and the Moluccas. Philip was also rewarded with a vast influx of New World silver in the 1580s, after the introduction of mercury into the smelting process, funding an increase in the silk and spice trades. Portugal's western coastline also provided ports with easier access to Northern Europe.

Analysis now suggests that the acquisition had negative as well as positive consequences. Geoffrey Scammell, in *The First Imperial Age: European Overseas Expansion C. 1400–1715* (1989), argues that the Portuguese empire proved a serious drain on the Spanish economy; defence costs became crippling, and there was little control of colonists in Brazil or traders in the East. A Council for India was not set up until six years after Philip's death, but it made no attempt to bring local peoples under Spanish control and soon became powerless and insolvent. The increased promise of funding encouraged Philip, whose grasp of cash flow was by his own admission extremely weak, to raise higher loans and embark on a forward policy against the heretics of Northern Europe. Philip's enemies concluded that there was safety in numbers and attack seemed the best form of defence. In the 1590s, Spain faced a three-pronged war against England, France and the United Provinces.

Dom Antonio: alternative claimant for the vacant throne of Portugal; illegitimate son of the brother of Portugal's previous ruler Cardinal Henry (great-uncle to Philip's nephew Sebastian, who was King until 1578).

Was Philip II's policy aggressively imperialist after 1583?

Did Philip II intend to establish a 'Universal Monarchy'?

In 1556 Philip himself informed his father, 'I have no claims to the territory of others,' yet many contemporaries feared Philip's attempt to establish a 'Universal Monarchy'. In 1581 a triumphal arch in Lisbon referred to 'the lord of the world', and a 1583 medal incorporated into the royal coat of arms the motto 'Non Sufficit Orbis' (the world is not enough). R. A. Stradling, in *Europe and the Decline of Spain* (1981), notes that with the acquisition of Portugal and its empire, Spain ruled 'the greatest aggregation of peoples, jurisdiction and wealth the world had ever seen'.

Many historians agree that Philip's conservative and defensive policy became aggressive imperialism after 1583. Henry Kamen, in *Philip of Spain* (1997), argues that 'Philip was not a conscious imperialist', he merely searched for security in moving outwards to the Atlantic, but admits, 'Every move by Spain looked like aggression, and it was easy to interpret Spanish policy as a lust for power.' Fernand Braudel, in *The Mediterranean and the Mediterranean World in the Age of Philip II* (1949), sees Philip's role as reactive rather than strategically planned, stating:

> Grand designs were revived less as a result of the personal desires of the sovereign than through force of circumstance.

A series of provocations by both sides turned the long-standing Anglo-Spanish alliance into tense hostility by the 1580s. Spain seized 10 of John Hawkins' privateering ships in San Juan de Ulloa (1567), causing a wave of English pamphlets condemning Philip's tyranny. Elizabeth retaliated by seizing a £40 000 Genoese loan en route to Alva's army when the ships sought shelter in Plymouth (1568). Tit-for-tat trade embargoes took place, causing ship confiscations in English and Spanish ports. Elizabeth drew diplomatically closer to the French, proposing a marriage alliance with the Duke of Anjou and later his younger brother Alençon. Philip's support of plots against Elizabeth, and his delight at the **Massacre of St Bartholomew** (1572), sent out a clear message, while Sir Francis Drake's circumnavigation of the globe in 1577–80, during which he attacked Nombre de Diós, exposed the vulnerability of the Spanish empire. Drake's lightning raids on Spanish ports gave him the fearsome reputation of 'El Draco'

Massacre of St Batholomew: French-Catholic massacre of 3000 Huguenots who were assembled in Paris en route to help the Dutch rebels. Copied by orgies of killing (perhaps 15 000 Huguenots) throughout France.

(the dragon), yet Elizabeth knighted him at Tilbury. Raleigh and Grenville attempted to colonise Virginia, directly threatening Spanish trade routes. Philip's 'Grand Strategy' allowed for defensive attack, as did Elizabeth I.

The Duke of Parma's military successes in the Netherlands coincided with the deaths of the rebel leaders, the Duke of Anjou and William of Orange (1584), forcing Elizabeth's intervention to aid the Dutch by the Treaty of Nonsuch (1585). This implicit declaration of war led Philip to begin preparations for the invasion of England – part of his 'Grand Strategy' of conserving and defending his Netherlands inheritance. Yet Reginald Trevor Davies, in *The Golden Century of Spain, 1501*–1621 (1937), writes:

> His ultimate objective was the domination of the British Isles and France by means of intervention in their religious struggle.

To the English, the Armada was the act of an aggressive imperialist.

The Armada controversy

Geoffrey Parker and Colin Martin, in *The Spanish Armada* (1988), support the 'messianic imperialism' of 'Grand Strategy', with a comment by the Duke of Medina Sidonia. He explained:

> 'The principal reason which has moved his Majesty to undertake this enterprise, is his desire to serve God, and to convert to His Church many peoples and souls who are now oppressed by the heretical enemies of the Catholic faith.'

Parker and Martin note the Jesuits aboard the fleet and those waiting as a taskforce in Flanders under Cardinal William Allen, who was to lead the new English Catholic state. They also note Philip's order that Parma must ensure religious toleration for Catholics in England. However, Henry Kamen, in *Spain's Road to Empire: The Making of a World Power, 1492–1763* (2003), argues to the contrary, saying:

> Philip never excluded religious coexistence as a political alternative, in the case of a successful invasion of England.

'The Armada was not primarily a religious crusade, for Philip was a realist, not a visionary,' concludes Geoffrey Woodward, in *Philip II* (1992). Geoffrey Parker, in *The Grand Strategy of Philip II* (1998), disagrees, arguing:

> ['Messianic vision'] led to the error of adopting unrealistic

policies, doing everything humanly possible to put them into effect and then relying on divine intervention to 'bridge the gap'.

Parker suggests Philip's 'cognitive rigidity' (Pierson's 'half-measure' or 'last-minute expedient') made him willing to cast caution to the winds, without making any contingency plans. In the same way that he had rejected policies other than war in dealing with the Dutch rebels, he refused to consider alternatives to the Armada, despite his commanders' misgivings. Fireships destroyed only 18 of the 130-strong fleet, but North Sea storms sank all but 60, which limped back to Spain. Parker concludes that Philip's persistence in a single approach for short-term gain turned to resignation at failure when it proved unworkable, rather than the search for an alternative policy. Peter Pierson's judgement, in *Philip II of Spain* (1975), seems appropriate: 'As an instrument of God's will, his diffidence belied God's trust.'

The Spanish Armada grouped off Calais (Cales), awaiting the rendezvous with Parma's army. Lord Henry Seymour's eastern squadron left its anchorage (top left) and sailed across the straits of Dover for the final assault on the Armada. Within hours, the Armada cut its anchors, panicked by a fireship attack.

Historians disagree widely on Philip's motives in 1588. 'The objective of this Armada is both the security of the Indies and the reconquest of the Netherlands,' said a royal secretary, quoted by Henry Kamen, in *Spain's Road to Empire: The Making of a World Power, 1492–1763* (2003). Katherine Brice, in 'Philip II: Northern Europe' in *Years of Renewal: European History 1470–1600* (1988), argues:

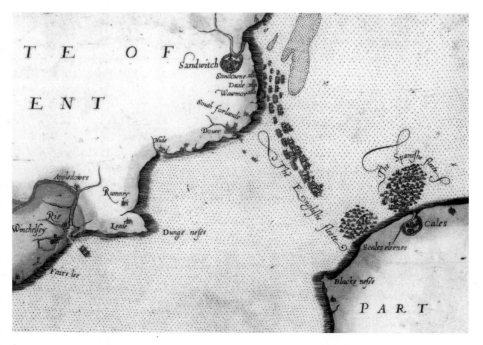

Religion was not the main factor in Philip's decision, although it was the one that Philip chose to emphasise. More important were political and economic factors.

In Geoffrey Woodward's view, in *Philip II* (1992), 'His priority was to stop the English from interfering in the Netherlands,' whereas R.A. Stradling, in *Europe and the Decline of Spain* (1981), considers *'reputación'* and *'conservación'* were at stake.

Parker's 'Grand Strategy' theory encompasses the full range of these historians' different explanations of the Armada – religious, economic, defensive, imperialist – all were elements of his 'Grand Strategy'. Dynastic imperialism was added by Mary Queen of Scots' recognition of Philip as heir to her English claim before her execution (1587). Philip was sure he had 'a divine mandate with respect to England'. He was confident that God would provide him with a miraculous victory against the heretic English, so that he could restore the Catholic faith there. In *The Spanish Armada* (1988), Geoffrey Parker and Colin Martin argue that Philip was the 'creator and absolute director of a coordinated plan, of which the Armada was an integral part, to strike a mortal blow to the heart of Tudor England'.

Did 'Grand Strategy' collapse in the 1590s?

The humiliation of the Armada defeat struck at Philip's providentialism, for God had favoured the heretic English. This, plus the Pope's refusal to contribute his promised one million ducats, reduced Philip's *'reputación'* to a low ebb. But the 'defensive' war widened. The death of the Duke of Anjou made the Huguenot Henry of Navarre heir to the French throne, committing Philip, in the Treaty of Joinville (1584), to aid the Catholic League. Henri III's assassination (1589) meant that Navarre would be king if Catholic Paris allowed his coronation. Philip's duty as 'Catholic King' was to prevent the loss of France for the Catholic faith. Furthermore, Henry might support the Dutch rebels, exposing the obedient Southern provinces to attack on two fronts. The anti-Spanish Pope Sixtus V commented caustically (1589):

> The King of Spain, as a temporal sovereign, is anxious above all to safeguard and increase his dominions. The preservation of the Catholic religion, which is the principal aim of the Pope, is only a pretext for His Majesty whose principal aim is the security and aggrandisement of his dominions.

Philip wrote a bad-tempered reply, rebuking the Pope for his inaction. Debt made the King adopt a 'wait-and-see' policy and, when forced to intervene militarily in France, he justified his action as conservation of the faith and defence of his lands. But to those who noticed that France 'lay at the heart of the Spanish monarchy', as a Spanish minister observed, Philip's intervention looked like aggressive territorial expansion.

Philip trusted that God would provide, despite his ministers' warnings of 'war without end, for which there are neither lives nor money sufficient'. Philip even suggested introducing an element of toleration in the Netherlands, at the expense of his *'reputación'*, but his need for papal approval prolonged the military stalemate there. The Duke of Parma reluctantly abandoned a potentially winning position in the Netherlands to successfully relieve Paris, under siege by Navarre's troops. To generations of Protestant historians, Philip's claim of the French crown for his daughter Isabella, in violation of **Salic law**, seemed aggressively imperialist. He pursued 'matrimonial imperialism', 'messianic imperialism', *'reputación'* and *'conservación'*, although Spaniards angrily protested that it was not in their national economic interest.

Salic law: the law excluding the female line from accession to the French crown.

'The Papacy believed Philip had confused what was best for the Church with what was best for Spain,' comments Geoffrey Woodward, in *Philip II* (1992). Yet harvest failure in 1593/4, high taxes, drought and famine compounded the misery of Spaniards. Parma's death (1592) from wounds received at Rouen, gave conduct of the Dutch War to Alva's brother-in-law Count Fuentes and the Archduke Ernst of Austria; neither a match for Maurice of Nassau, who was a brilliant military commander. He took advantage of weak Spanish troops to advance southwards into the obedient provinces. 'Domino theory' re-emerged as Philip's three enemies joined forces in the Triple Alliance (1596), formally recognising the rebel Dutch provinces as a nation state.

Politique: a politician who puts the good of the state before religion.

The **politique** Henry of Navarre abjured his heresy (July 1593), converted to Catholicism, receiving Pope Clement VIII's pardon (1595), and entered Paris to be crowned Henry IV, saying, 'Paris is well worth a Mass!' He then declared war on Spain. Meanwhile, Philip, showing his accustomed 'cognitive rigidity' and lack of contingency plans at a time of crisis, persisted in Isabella's claim even though Frenchmen preferred a national candidate. Two further unsuccessful Armadas, another bankruptcy (1596) and the death, in childbirth, of his daughter Catalina Duchess of Savoy (1597), devastated the dying King.

Philip's reign closed in disaster and defeat at the Treaty of Vervins

Twelve-Year Truce:
ceasefire between the
Spanish and Dutch for 12
years (1609–21).

(1598), described by the French as 'most advantageous' and by Fuentes as 'shameful'. Desperate to achieve peace, Philip granted limited autonomy jointly to Albert and Isabella in the Southern Netherlands, athough the Dutch stalemate continued until the **Twelve-Year Truce.** 'No surrender' remained the strategy there, until Dutch independence was finally recognised (1648). Philip's 'messianic vision' had saddled him with a war that could not be won or ended in his lifetime. Geoffrey Parker, in *The Grand Strategy of Philip II* (1998), assesses Philip's success:

> In the Mediterranean, as in the Americas, the King achieved most of his policy goals; in the Netherlands and against England he did not, thus beginning the decline of Spain as a great power. … Small events played a disproportionate part in frustrating a 'Grand Strategy' that, on the face of it, stood an excellent chance of success.

'Grand Strategy' on paper became 'crisis management' in practice.

 ## Was Philip II's foreign policy 'Grand Strategy' or crisis management?

1. Read the following extract and answer the question.

   'Surely Philip could have exploited the serious weaknesses of Spain's enemies to better advantage: Germany divided uneasily between Protestant and Catholic; England ruled by a woman who, although an adroit politician, lacked a clear successor and needed to accommodate a large religious minority; above all France, seriously weakened by repeated religious wars. Yet despite these uniquely favourable international circumstances Philip failed both to preserve what he had inherited and to achieve the dynastic and confessional goals that he had set.'

   (G. Parker, *The Grand Strategy of Philip II*, Yale University Press, 1998.)

   Using the information in the extract above, and from this section, explain why Philip II failed to achieve his foreign policy objectives.

2. 'Philip II's foreign policy lacked consistency.' Do you agree?

Philip II: an assessment

Character and administration

Philip valued reputation above all else. Although he is no longer considered a tyrant, he is either portrayed as an indecisive, weak bureaucrat or a man obsessed by messianic vision. His authoritarian character was reminiscent of Ferdinand the Catholic, the inspiration for Machiavelli's *Prince*, who judged it 'better to be feared than loved'. Philip was an authoritarian, who was shielded by his papers from the reality of power, shrouded in secrecy and mistrust, and restricted by inherited structures and personal weaknesses. He would never give in, as his father had in 1556, but intransigence was his greatest weakness not his greatest strength.

The champion of the Catholic Church

Philip was powerless to change the engrained attitudes of Spanish society, which he himself embodied. Although driven by messianic vision, he was ineffective in reforming Spain's national Church and undermined his role as champion of the Counter-Reformation by national interest and disputes with the papacy. The myth of the Inquisition earned him an evil reputation and inspired fear, but its bureaucrats failed to censor or impose orthodoxy on a diverse society. The Inquisition's political, cultural and social role remains disputed.

Foreign strategy

The strengths and weaknesses of Philip's autocracy are apparent in his conduct of foreign policy. On the one hand, he proactively pursued a diverse range of inherited strategies, bound by an unshakeable belief that God's will was consistent with his own. On the other hand, he inconsistently and reactively followed his range of ambitions, sometimes defending and sometimes attacking for defence, but generally he hoped to enhance reputation and faith. When events, his global inheritance, micromanagement or bankruptcy caused crisis, he persisted with ineffective, even failed, strategies.

Philip II's legacy

Though considered the 'zenith' of Spanish greatness, Philip II's reign ended in humiliating defeat. The façade was built on fortuitous inheritance, mortgaged New World silver, a crumbling economy and inefficient autocratic administration. The incompetent Philip III handed power to Lerma, who conserved it through peace, followed by Olivares, who resumed the Dutch War. As New World silver dried up, Bourbon France, under Philip's great-grandson Louis XIV, emerged as the dominant European power at the end of the 17th century. Habsburg 'matrimonial imperialism' culminated in the abnormal and impotent Carlos II, whose death inaugurated Bourbon rule of Spain.

Further reading

Texts specifically designed for students

Kamen, H. *Golden Age Spain* (Macmillan, 1988)

Kilsby, J. *Spain: Rise and Decline, 1474–1643* (Hodder & Stoughton, 1986)

McKinnon-Bell, D. *Philip II (Access to History in Depth)* (Hodder & Stoughton, 2001)

Parker, G. *The World is Not Enough: The Imperial Vision of Philip II of Spain* (Baylor University Press, 2001)

Woodward, G. *Philip II* (Longman Seminar Studies, 1992)

Texts for more advanced study

Darby, G. (ed.) *The Origins and Development of the Dutch Revolt* (Routledge, 2001) provides clear summaries of events, historiography and analysis of themes within the Dutch Revolt.

Kamen, H. *Philip of Spain* (Yale University Press, 1997) offers a compelling, intimate and persuasive portrayal of Philip II's character and life.

Kamen, H. *Spain's Road to Empire: The Making of a World Power, 1492–1763* (Penguin, 2003) provides an analysis of the impact of the global empire on Spain.

Kamen, H. *The Spanish Inquisition: A Historical Revision* (Weidenfeld & Nicolson, 1997) is an influential study that caused historians to rethink the role and impact of the Spanish Inquisition.

Parker, G. *Philip II* (Cardinal Books, 1979) is a very readable biography with a balanced portrayal of the King, if rather incomplete in the light of recent research.

Parker, G. *The Grand Strategy of Philip II* (Yale University Press, 1998) offers a comparative analysis of management structures and foreign strategies with illustrative case studies, including the Armada and the Dutch Revolt.

Pierson, P. *Philip II of Spain* (Thames & Hudson, 1975) provides a detailed and perceptive history of the King and his reign with evaluation of his policies.

Rawlings, H. *Church, Religion and Society in Early Modern Spain* (Palgrave Macmillan, 2002) is a readable and strongly-structured analysis with new insights into the interaction between the Church and the people.

Index